STUDENT
CONGRESS

Linda L. Oddo

New Trier High School
Winnetka, Illinois

Thomas B. McClain

New Trier High School
Winnetka, Illinois

 **National Textbook Company**
NTC a division of *NTC Publishing Group* • Lincolnwood, Illinois USA

The authors and the publisher wish to thank the National Forensic League for the use of the National Student Congress transcript in Chapter One.

Published by National Textbook Company, a division of NTC Publishing Group.
©1994 by NTC Publishing Group, 4255 West Touhy Avenue,
Lincolnwood (Chicago), Illinois 60646-1975 U.S.A.
Manufactured in the United States of America.
Library of Congress Catalog Card Number: 93-83537

3 4 5 6 7 8 9 0 VP 9 8 7 6 5 4 3 2 1

Contents

Preface

In 1938 the National Forensic League (NFL) sponsored the first National Student Congress in Wooster, Ohio, with the stated purpose of giving high school students actual practice in self-government. The congress was a great success and a call was made to have regular Student Congress competitions at the NFL district level. Although there have been changes in rules and procedures over the years, the goal of Student Congress participation has remained constant—training for active participation in the life of the nation. It is a credit to the NFL leaders that they realized that argument is a great equalizer and that the democratic process can be sustained only through informed citizen involvement in the important issues of governance. In *Decision by Debate*, Douglas Ehninger and Wayne Brockriede tell us that "when men [sic] are called on to make choices or decisions, they proceed in one of two ways. Either they examine the available evidence and survey accepted motives and values to discover what conclusions are warranted, or, disregarding evidence and values, they leap to a conclusion impulsively on the basis of desire, superstition, or prejudice." This book is intended for those who believe that logical decisions are preferable to emotional decisions.

Student Congress: Preparing for Legislative Debate reflects our effort to adapt basic argumentation theory to the demands of debating controversial topics in a legislative setting. We have drawn on our experience as teachers, coaches, researchers, and observers of Student Congress competition for the argumentation theory; for the suggestions about how students can learn library skills that will allow them to access and evaluate information; and for practical advice on learning the rules of parliamentary procedure, preparing legislative research packets, and developing deliberative speeches.

Because public issues affect the lives of every citizen, it is imperative that students become critical thinkers capable of advocating their beliefs in a public forum. The ability to use arguments effectively is important both for self-growth and for the preservation of an open society. The demands of a democratic society require that students be able to recognize and analyze controversial topics, construct arguments to support and defend positions they take on these topics, and attack effectively the positions and arguments of those who disagree. To this end we have included in this text two chapters that discuss practical reasoning as applied to persuasive communication in a legislative setting, one chapter that reflects our belief that knowledge gained from extensive research is an indispensable part of thoughtful decision making, and three chapters that contain useful advice for student competitors. An actual Student Congress debate, a student-prepared authorship speech, a glossary, and appendix materials are included for study.

Although this book is intended primarily for students who participate in Student Congress competition, we think it can serve as an important supplement in English and social studies courses in which current issues are part of the curriculum and the development of critical thinking skills is emphasized. Students who participate in model congresses, model United Nations, and other state and national conventions that are organized to give students legislative experience will find this book beneficial.

We conclude by thanking those individuals who contributed to the writing of this book. Alice Basoms, New Trier High School librarian, offered invaluable advice and assisted us in writing Chapter Three, and Ray Ledinsky provided us with materials for Chapter Six. We are indebted to the teachers, coaches, colleagues, and students who helped shape our thinking, and especially to the authors of the argumentation and debate texts that we have used for the past two decades: Douglas Ehninger and Wayne Brockriede, *Decision by Debate*; J. W. Patterson and David Zarefsky, *Contemporary Debate*; and Barbara Warnick and Edward S. Inch, *Critical Thinking and Communication: The Use of Reason in Argument*. We also are grateful for the contributions of the teachers and Student Congress coaches of the Northern Illinois District of the

National Forensic League. Their efforts to expand the scope of Student Congress competition and their willingness to experiment to improve the activity provided us with useful insights.

We offer our sincere thanks to our secretaries, Teresa Costabile and Rose Fleming, for the many hours they spent assisting us in the preparation of this document. In addition, we wish to thank Nina Lynn and Hilerre Kirsch, who assisted in the creation of the Teacher's Manual. We also appreciate the encouragement offered by the staff at National Textbook Company during the writing of this book.

Finally, we wish to thank James Copeland, executive secretary of the National Forensic League, for allowing us to reproduce the Table of Most Frequently Used Parliamentary Motions from the NFL *Student Congress Manual* and to record and transcribe "A Resolution Concerning Japanese Trade," the debate that took place at an NFL National Student Congress. We also appreciate the materials supplied by Albert Odom, editor of *The Rostrum*, on the history of NFL Student Congress competition.

L. L. O.
T. B. Mc.

CHAPTER 1

The Use of Reason in a Legislative Debate

It is our contention that the study of argumentation is fundamental to success in legislative debate. Our purpose in this text is to provide useful information for students when controversial topics are debated. We do not pretend that the material we present is new. Our goal is to carefully detail and illustrate the topics essential to deliberative debate. Policy issues about which people generally argue are complex; they subsume questions of meaning, fact, and value. To be successful students must weigh the available facts, make reasonable interpretations, offer judgments, and defend the predictions that they make.

Studying how arguments function in a legislative assembly will enable you to research controversial topics successfully, locate evidence to support or attack positions, present well-organized speeches for or against a proposed course of action, evaluate and criticize arguments of others, and respond to attacks on positions that you advocate.

Before moving to a discussion of an argument model and the component parts of an argument, we include a transcript of an actual Student Congress debate. We will use examples from this debate to amplify our discussion of argument in this chapter.

1

Transcript of an NFL National Student Congress Debate

The following is a transcript of a debate that took place at a National Forensic League National Student Congress. The participants in this debate were the top twenty-four senators selected to participate in the Super Session.

The transcript is a verbatim account of the debate. Only superfluous motions, minor flaws in delivery, and the participants' names are omitted.

MODERATOR:

Motion to open debate on Resolution F, "A Resolution Concerning Japanese Trade," is before you. Is there a second? Aye. After a reading of the resolution we will begin the debate on Resolution F.

A RESOLUTION CONCERNING JAPANESE TRADE*

1   Whereas: The United States has a trade deficit of 185
2   billion dollars with just Japan, and

---

*Note: All bills and resolutions submitted for competition must be double spaced. See pages 85–90 for standard formats.

3   Whereas: It is the trade restrictions, import taxes, and
4   government-subsidized businesses which create an unfair market
5   in Japan for U.S. products, and
6   Whereas: It is these antitrade actions that inflate the
7   cost of American goods in Japan and not poor quality which
8   reduce sales, and
9   Whereas: Specific items are not allowed to be imported
10   because the Japanese government knows that American goods
11   would outsell their Japanese counterparts, and
12   Whereas: The Japanese trade restrictions inherently
13   produce an unfair and unequal opportunity to benefit from
14   Japanese consumers, therefore,
15   Be it resolved by the National Forensic League's National
16   Student Congress that the United States shall implement the
17   same trade measures that the Japanese Government has been
18   taking against the U.S. until such time that the Japanese lift
19   their own unfair antitrade practices.

MODERATOR:
Is there an affirmative speech?

SENATOR #1:
I have such a speech. Recently seeing George Bush lying in the lap of the
Japanese prime minister and being sick, it was kind of symbolic to me
when I looked at it. Number one, it showed the position Americans were
in with the Japanese, and number two, it showed how sick Americans can
get about Japanese trade. The U.S. has a major economic problem on its
hands today. We are constantly engaging in free trade policies with other
countries that are lacking in doing the same. For example, in 1987, American farmers lost over one billion dollars in Europe because of unfair
trade. But today we are not fighting the ECC [sic], there's another country. That country is Japan, and if this piece of legislation passes it will be
a great day for American workers, America, and business!

There are many problems with our system of free trade with other countries and Japan. As a February 1991 issue of *The New York Times* reported,
we allow unlimited numbers of autos to be sold in the United States while
we are being locked out of the Japanese market. This discrimination sti-
fles competition and makes a joke of free trade. In January 1987 Japan set
up their first surplus trade in which we were not allowed to come into their
country, and what happened? Our deficit shot up and hit a record high.
Since many of the goods we send to Japan have high tariffs on them we

cannot make the revenue enough to pay off the trade deficit and we are sort of stuck at a standstill. Also, the ways to correct the problem of free trade have caused us to sell products that cost more because the Japanese are able to hire workers that are willing to do better work, but accept lower wages. But our workers want to do the work they want to do regardless of how good it is and in the process want higher wages.

Recently our government instituted the "luxury tax." Now the luxury tax is exempt to other countries that want to bring these products in such as cigarettes and wine and the big boats. When they sell those to us they are exempt of it. So, in our own country our own businesses selling these luxury items are being held back while foreign ones are coming in. Today, the U.S. has a 185 billion dollar trade deficit with the Japanese. This number is extremely large and ridiculous. Despite the U.S.'s higher production of cars and the Japanese's lower production, a Michigan study predicts that the deficit will worsen. The automobile trade deficit is predicted to go up to 47%, to 45.7 billion in 1994. How can a country like ours that produces so much fall so far behind? In a poll by *Newsweek* magazine in 1992, 67% of the people surveyed said that unfair trade practices by the Japanese were our reason for being behind in trade. American businesses are being cheated out of their opportunity and competitiveness and it's cutting jobs! So, this gives a right for us to uphold what we believe we should do that the Japanese are doing. So therefore, I urge you to pass this legislation.

MODERATOR:
Questions?

SENATOR #2:
Senator, regardless of the car issue, isn't it true that the Japanese can produce a car for the same price regardless of workers' wages that is a higher quality deemed so by American critics?

SENATOR #1:
The Japanese have been able to produce a car at a lower price and is of good production, and they are paying their workers less for it. That is where the laziness factor came in—that our workers want more to do less.

MODERATOR:
Other questions?

SENATOR #3:
Isn't it true that in the past Japanese goods would be more and Americans could then raise prices?

SENATOR #1:
No, it's not true. What this is attempting to do, I believe, is by us agreeing to put up a front and say, "Hey, we're not going to take any more from the Japanese," they may get scared because we accept the majority of their goods, they'll get scared and drop the majority of their tariffs down, maybe not away, but drop it down, which will allow for more American products to be distributed worldwide.

SENATOR #4:
Senator, isn't it true that many American cars are not suited toward the Japanese needs and this is why the cars are not popular in Japan?

SENATOR #1:
This is true in the sense that even the Japanese government tries to make it so that United States' products, and other countries' products, won't work within Japan so that the Japanese will be forced to buy Japanese products. This went against the General Agreement on Trade and Tariffs [GATT] agreement agreed to between the Japanese and Americans in which it said that if they did such a thing they could be retaliated against by the United States.

SENATOR #5:
Wouldn't a lack of Japanese investment in our nation hurt our economy?

SENATOR #1:
It all depends on whether this will lessen the flow of Japanese investment or not. I don't think even if we do drop it down that Japanese investment can be lessened. Actually, I think the Free Trade Agreement, or even high tariffs, could bring more in.

MODERATOR:
Thank you, Senator. Are there any motions? Hearing none, we're in line for a negative speaker. Senator #2, do you accept such a speech?

SENATOR #2:
Yes, Sir. A modern philosopher offers us the following lines. "The moves you make you make for yourself. The things you do you do for yourself. The means you use aren't meant to confuse, and although they do, they're the ones I would choose." Pointing out that in today's society there are many things that confuse the American public that are done by higher levels of government, specifically in the Japanese area. We can see that the Japanese

people have been consistently able to produce higher-quality products at a lower cost which in the eyes of an American is very confusing because we do not understand why a country so far away and so small compared to ourselves can manage to outdo us time and time again. But we look very specifically at the car industry, the industry that would be most affected by this piece of legislation, we can look toward the American analysis, *Car and Driver*, and realize that in January 1992, *Car and Driver* pointed out after a two-year study that regardless of wages even though the average Japanese auto worker earns $10 per hour, and the average American auto worker earns $30 per hour, regardless of that statistic, the Japanese can produce a car at a lower cost that is deemed by the American public of higher quality. If we look very carefully at Line 6 (of the resolution) where it begins the third Whereas clause, we can see that it is these antitrade actions that have raised the cost of American goods in Japan and not poor quality which have reduced sales. That is a blatant contradiction and is proven incorrect by simple American statistics and studies. If the Americans are willing to admit this wrong, then there is a blatant conflict in the concept and logic of this bill. But, even to move on, we can see as Franklin D. Roosevelt said, ''The greatest pleasure offered by life is the option to work hard at something that is worth doing.'' The Americans are not working hard at the things that they feel are worth doing. If you ask an average American auto worker, as *The New York Times* did at a Ford plant in the Midwest, one responded by saying, ''The damned [Japanese] need to stop working so hard so we can catch up.'' Now obviously that's not the general mentality of the American worker, but it does show the trend that we feel almost oppressed by the superiority of the Japanese technology. Some might argue that the technology that the Japanese utilized was given to them by us, as in the form of the CD, but that only proves that if we had the technology before them and they used it to higher reaches, it is obvious that they are willing to work harder, more quickly and more efficiently, and so thus, by simply imposing legislation that is going to hurt our own economy, it is not realistic to ask the American people to suffer on the basis of their own laziness. Simply put, we need to reemphasize the work ethic and take pride in what we do and not what the Japanese are doing. ''Nothing will come of nothing,'' as it states from an eloquent philosopher.

MODERATOR:
Thank you, Senator. Any questions?

SENATOR #6:
Yes, Senator #2, isn't it true that even with import tariffs Americans prefer Japanese articles even if they are high quality?

SENATOR #2:
That's exactly true! Even if Americans kept our cars at a lower price and a higher cost of Japanese cars, we can see that the people who buy these cars would much rather have higher quality, higher efficiency and all that comes along with it.

SENATOR #7:
Isn't it true that most people in the United States would much rather have a BMW than an American car?

SENATOR #2:
That's the point that was earlier addressed. The fact is we would much rather pay for convenience, and if convenience costs less why would you choose something that isn't?

MODERATOR:
Thank you, Senator. Are there any motions? Hearing none, we're in line for an affirmative speech.

SENATOR #8:
Hello, Senators. There is something which I don't understand, which gives this debate serious racist undertones. He [Senator #2] quoted a worker who said, ''Those damned [Japanese], why don't they stop working so hard, and let us catch up?'' Some may look at this resolution as a resolution with racist undertones. However, I urge you to look past that because I am not speaking to the point of view of a racist, for I can empathize with the Japanese. This has nothing to do with economic inferiority. This has nothing to do with trying to equalize our economies. The real purpose behind this legislation is perhaps political. Now I urge you to look at this economic issue from a political point of view. First of all, look at the trained society that Japan has created out of its cultural heritage. A notable Japanese businessman, Kobashi, says, ''It's very deep seated and twisted and complicated. Still we feel the presence of some controlling agent. We can't quite specify who or what so we are not frank. Even speaking among ourselves sometimes we use the *hon*

ne, generally felt element, the speech for our own people, but when we speak to foreigners often we still speak in *ta te mae,* the false front. Sometimes we are relatively relaxed, free to make any kind of comment or speech, but we suddenly shrink and begin hiding ourselves.''

In other words, Japan cannot face America sincerely. It's not a racist issue, it's merely an issue of a different cultural background, and this has inhibited an equality in the new global economies which are developing today. This trained society is why some sort of tariff removal is necessary among our two nations. Second of all, let's look at the Japanese economy now and the way it was fifty years ago. Historically, fledgling economies always impose trade restrictions. The Japanese economy fifty years ago was just starting out changing from its economy based in the last century and based on the war effort, based into a capitalistic economy in which they used the United States model. The United States itself imposed similar restrictions as its economy was developing. But the Japanese economy is no longer fledgling as we can clearly see. The Japanese economy can clearly hold its own and, therefore, trade restrictions are no longer necessary. Finally, let's look at the global economy in which we live today, in which these sort of trade restrictions inhibit the sort of free trade between nations that promotes the advancement of all our societies. Now what I would really like to say is that plainly this is not an issue of downturn economics because Japan is not the largest market in the world. What money can we really gain by selling products to the Japanese? Perhaps not much, but to equalize our influences in a global economy in global politics, I believe, this resolution addresses.

MODERATOR:
Senator, will you yield for questions?

SENATOR #9:
Senator, would it be more prudent to build new markets instead of closing others?

SENATOR #2:
Yes, it would.

SENATOR #10:
How can you narrow the space in economic politics?

SENATOR #2:
Oh, if we divorce the world's economics and politics, then clearly the two are related, economics influences politics, and politics influences

economics. But let us make sure that our economics and politics are not biased.

MODERATOR:

Thank you, Senator. Are there any motions? Hearing none, we are in line for a negative speech.

SENATOR #7:

I have such a speech. Ladies and gentlemen, I want to ask you a question. Is anyone here a businessman? Does anyone here own a company? Does anyone in here have an idea what it is to be a businessman? Well, if you don't, how can you be in favor of this bill or this resolution? Ladies and gentlemen, I am going to tell you one thing, please—would you let business do business! Ladies and gentlemen—one of the risks people take when they want to make money, when they want to succeed, if they take risks in the business market, sometimes it's fair, sometimes it's not fair, sometimes they have to look for new ways, look for alternatives. They have to take the risk. If you are trying to tell them what to do, trying to make the choices for them, you're not letting them do what they want to do—business. What was brought up before. Question, Is it better to close a market or seek new ones? Ladies and gentlemen, if we cut off Japan, we're closing our market. If we cut off Japan, we're cutting off any type of trade we can have there. In other words, you're going to the businessman and you're saying, Businessman, you can't have any part of Japan, you can't try to take the risk to sell your products, make them cheaper, make them better. According to *Business Week*, April 6, 1992, a humorist once observed that the Japanese have the audacity to sell us good cars at good prices. Why should that make us mad? Also, another illogical concept running through here is a rumor about the trade deficit. Simply, this resolution does not have any idea what the trade deficit is. Again, according to *Business Week*, the same issue, according to Alan S. Blinder, an economist, he said that there are myths. No. 1—Trade deficits do not cause unemployment. No. 2—Our trade deficit has almost gone away. And No. 3—Our trade problems are not made in Japan. This is a fact! Ladies and gentlemen, to sum up, the trade deficit is not our problem! It's not made in Japan! It's not affecting at all to the lengths that some of you are trying to make out and if you want business to succeed, if you want to let the economy grow, please—let business do business!

MODERATOR:

Thank you, Senator. Do any of you have questions?

SENATOR #1:
How can we let business do business—but Japan won't even let them do what they want to do because they're not opening up?

SENATOR #7:
The problem that we are having with Japan is that Japan is cheaper. They have the sense of competition, and as the other question pointed out, why should we close that market? Why should we close out any barrier that we have to make some money?

SENATOR #11:
Was the senator aware that according to the January 4 issue of *The Economist*, the 1991 trade deficit will be only four billion dollars due to a record number of exports?

SENATOR #7:
Yes, I was.

MODERATOR:
Are there any motions? Hearing none, we are in line for an affirmative speaker. Senator #12, will you accept a speech?

SENATOR #12:
Yes. Fellow Senators, I believe it was Pat Buchanan who put it best in a campaign speech in Atlanta in 1992, when he held up a picture of a mushroom cloud when he said—built in America by lazy unskilled workers and tested in Japan. Americans, fellow Senators, there are a lot of racial tensions when we talk about trade with Japan. There are a lot of tensions when we talk about this issue we are looking at today—but let's look at what we're doing when we pass this type of resolution. We're sending the right message. We're not closing American markets—we're not opening new Japanese markets *per se*, we're not stifling the American economy, we're simply sending a message. We're saying that we want to open those markets. It's very important when we look at a number of issues that have been brought up today. Jim Impatico, U.S. economist, points out, "In the past the competition was between a command economy and a market economy, but now it's with capitalism itself." And that's very important. We have no shift as the previous speaker was talking about in our global economic policy. There is a new global economic policy that is evolving and it is between capitalist markets, not between command economies and market economies. That's very important to remember. It also was in *U.S. News and World Report*, a cartoon—it said, I'll scratch your

back if you scratch mine and it had a very big Japanese sumo wrestler and a very small Uncle Sam. The Uncle Sam could in no way scratch the sumo wrestler's back, whereas the sumo wrestler could take his little pinky finger and scratch Uncle Sam into the dirt. It's very important that we even up these types of markets. It's very important that we send the right message! America's technology is second to none! We demonstrated this in the Gulf War, we demonstrated this with our military might, there is no reason why America's technology cannot compete in the same market as the Japanese market. Let's look at some of the other arguments the other senators have brought up. It says we are going to lessen our economy—we're going to stifle our businesses, that simply isn't true. Not with this resolution anyway. Because we're simply sending the message to Japan, if you open your markets, our markets will remain open. If you don't open your markets we're closing our markets down and I think that's going to open some eyes in Japan. It's also important to bring up that when a fellow senator brought up that economic policy is made to confuse Americans and that a lot of Americans don't understand economic policy—well the plain fact is this is a political issue and President Bush is playing a political game. He's simply appeasing the Japanese prime minister so he can be reelected. I think it's very interesting to see how much the Japanese contribute to President Bush's campaign. And when another senator talks about letting business do business, well they can't because the markets are closed, and therefore, I strongly urge you to pass this type of resolution.

MODERATOR:
Thank you, Senator. Will you yield for questions?

SENATOR #12:
Yes.

SENATOR #8:
Senator, isn't it true that we aren't likely to cut up the Japanese market if we are willing and able to take these measures?

SENATOR #12:
Yes, Senator, that's true, and that's why we ought to pass this resolution.

SENATOR #2:
Isn't it true that according to *New England Publications of Science and Technology*, microchip technology we use in our military missiles was beamed from Japan?

SENATOR #12:
Sir, I wouldn't know, I've never read that article.

MODERATOR:
Thank you. Are there any motions? Hearing none, we're in line for a negative speech. Senator #11, will you make such a speech?

SENATOR #11:
Yes. I have received a lot of jokes from a rural state, Alabama, but I will admit that I am very familiar with cows. Everyone here should know that cows do indeed practice protectionist policies. Whenever there is the slightest hint of danger a group of cows will huddle in a circle to prevent anyone else from getting in. Yet, despite this we now continue to milk cows for all their worth. If the United States establishes such a protectionist policy Japan will continue to milk us for all we're worth. Some senators have got up here and stated that Japan is not allowing us to do business, and that Japan's markets are closed. Frankly, Senators, this is simply not true. According to the December 30 *National Review*, Japan is the second largest importer of American goods with 49 billion dollars a year they're injecting into our economy. The Japanese spend $395 per person on American goods, while Americans only spend $359 per person on Japanese goods. Japan devoted 1.7% of its gross national product on American goods and we only devoted 1.6% of ours. Moreover, Japan's trade surplus has dropped 27% since its peak in 1987, while American exports to Japan have increased more than to any other nation in the world. Why is this? According to the March 2, 1992, *U.S. News and World Report*, Japan's tariff for industrial products is 2.6%. America's, in case anyone is curious, is 3%, and according to the World Bank, Japan's non-tariff barriers such as quotas and licenses are comparable to America's. Senators, if we are to enact this bill, we are actually lowering our trade restrictions against Japan. Which is of course perfectly fine to pursue more free trade instead of protectionist policies. According to economist Henry George, what protection teaches us to do to ourselves at peace is what our enemies seek to do to us in times of war. By keeping other countries out we are preventing our own economy from working the way it should. According to economist Samuelson, who was on the Reagan Council of Economic Advisers, and an economist at Harvard [sic], "An ill-designed tariff or quota will reduce a nation's real income by making imports more expensive and making the entire world less productive. A policy of free trade is the only policy to pursue." Moreover, we have learned from lessons in the past

that a protectionist policy can do nothing but hurt America. The Smoot-Hawley Act of the 1930s established higher tariffs. The result—retaliation and lower world trade in 1939 than in 1914. In 1984, restrictions on Japanese steel saved the U.S. 17,000 jobs in the steel market, yet cost us 54,000 jobs in other markets. Protectionist policies can only hurt us. Free trade can only help us and the situation is beneficial to America anyway. For this reason—vote negative.

SENATOR #8:
Question: Isn't it true that, as I pointed out, Japan is closer to free trade policies than we are anyway?

SENATOR #11:
Their tariffs are lower and their other restrictions are comparable to ours. Perhaps that's the reason it's more successful and they don't pay their workers as much, but I don't think anyone is willing to lower the minimum wage rate in America simply to become more competitive.

MODERATOR:
Thank you. Any motions? Hearing none, we are in for an affirmative speech. Senator #13, will you accept this speech?

SENATOR #13:
There is a little comical fictional story about George Bush. He was fishing in Kennebunkport, Maine, and there was a strong wind and he got a tug on the line and fell overboard. He was in the water for two minutes and when they pulled him out he was comatose. He fell into a coma for a number of years. When he finally awoke he said [to Dan Quayle] "Dan, what's happening—are you president?" He said, "Yes, I'm president, and I turned out to be better than anyone ever thought I would be."
    "How's productivity?"
    "About 40%, inflation is low."
    And George Bush goes—"What else is going on? How much does it cost to send a postcard?"
    "Oh, around 300 yen."
    This obviously shows the animosity between the United States and Japan. It shows the fears, the deep-seated fears that many Americans have about all the investment that we allow from Japan and none of which Japan allows us to put in their country. They have strict trade barriers, noneven tariffs, they close out whole markets to the United States while we allow them unlimited trade. First of all, I think it's

important that we look at what is the road to free trade. A *New Republic* article from June 26, 1991, quoted Lee Iacocca as saying ''the road to free trade first started out with equality in trade.'' When there are trade barriers in existence we are not on that road, we are taking a step backwards. To be put on the road to free trade we have to start out with equality. If they have tariffs against us, we must have tariffs against them, and lower them in combination. Senator #11 speaks of how that in trade with Japan that they are actually better than we are in allowing as much imports. However, we must realize that most of the imports are raw materials that the Japanese use in constructing finished goods to then be exported to the United States. Fighting on this kind of unlevel playing field would be perhaps as Senator #23 would say, trying to win a football game playing defense the whole game with unlimited time. It would be impossible. There is no way the United States can win this. That is why we need to pass this piece of legislation because the United States is falling behind. For reasons of economic growth our United States workers can work as hard as they can, however, if we do not have the market in Japan and we allow unfettered imports into our country there is nothing they can do, there is nothing that the producers of the products can do. What would happen if we pass this piece of legislation in the United States Congress would be startling. We would have increased competition between our own companies. They would have newfound markets. New empty spaces in the electronics and the car industry where we could now take first in our own country as rightly we should. It would decrease United States dependence on Japan and make us a better nation as a whole. For these reasons, I believe that we should pass this piece of legislation because once and for all we would have to be fighting a fair fight, a fight we could win.

MODERATOR:
Senator #13, will you yield?

SENATOR #13:
Yes.

SENATOR #14:
You said that most of what the Japanese get from us is raw materials. Do you realize that according to *The New York Times*, last year 64% of U.S. exports to Japan were manufactured goods?

SENATOR #13:
What is the other percentage? Whereas the other percentage is obviously

in raw materials while we do not import any raw materials from them and only receive finished goods.

MODERATOR:
Any motions? None! We are in line for a negative speech. Senator #14, do you accept such a speech?

SENATOR #14:
Senators, in urging you to negate this legislation I'd like to start off by telling you why this legislation is coming about. First of all, right now we are in a recession and we are having economic troubles in the United States. And the Bush administration is looking for an easy way out and an excuse. According to *The New York Times* in December 1991, the Bush administration is under pressure to take more aggressive action on trade partly because industries suffering from foreign competition are reluctant to give generously to the president's reelection campaign. You see the major reason this kind of legislation is coming about is due to the fact that it's election time and the president wants to make things look better so he is looking for an easy excuse to our problem. The second reason is because of anti-Japanese sentiment, and the major reason we have this sentiment is because Prime Minister Kiichi Miyazawa said Americans were lazy. According to *The New York Times*, he is mistranslated by the American press. He did not actually say that the Americans were lazy. So, this anti-Japanese sentiment is coming from the American press, not necessarily coming from the Japanese themselves. In urging you to negate this legislation I would like to go into several key points. First of all, supply and demand! The Japanese do not have a big demand for American products. There are several reasons. First of all, because the cars and the restrictions in Japan about cars are so different from the cars we make here in America. And there is a big problem. If there is no demand and supply, of course, there is going to be a problem with them buying from us. Second of all, I would like to go on to the point that restrictions will backfire. Restrictions aren't always good and do not always help the economy. According to *Current Issues*, published by the U.S. Closeup Program, most economists agree that trade restrictions do not increase the jobs in a country and only save jobs at a high cost. Moreover, trade restrictions can backfire and lead to higher prices for domestic products because domestic companies no longer need to keep their prices low to compete with imports. My next point, and I think the most important point here is, What is an American car? Over and over we have people up here debating that we need to buy more Ameri-

can cars. According to a *New York Times* article on what is an American car, the Ford Probe is built in Michigan by Mazda. The Plymouth Laser is built in Illinois by Mitsubishi. The Geo Prizm is built in California by Toyota. The Mercury Tracer is imported from Mexico. Chrysler vans are imported from Canada. Geo Metro is imported from Japan. So what you see is most of the American cars are in actuality not American cars. And my final point here is that the Japanese are helping the American economy. In the past decade Japanese automakers have transferred the production of 40% of their U.S. sales to America. This cost more than six billion dollars and created 39,000 jobs. I now yield to questions.

MODERATOR:
Thank you, Senator.

SENATOR #15:
Yes, Senator, you reported that Japanese officials didn't say that we were lazy, what actually did they say?

SENATOR #14:
The article did not go into details of it.

SENATOR #16:
If an American company like Chevrolet has a foreign company build the car for them and we buy that car, [don't] the final dollars still come back to this country?

SENATOR #14:
What is the question?

SENATOR #16:
If we buy a car even though it was made by a foreign company, if it was produced by an American company, [don't] the final dollars still come back to this country?

SENATOR #14:
A percentage, but a small percentage.

MODERATOR:
Thank you, Senator. Are there any motions?

SENATOR #17:
I move to lay this resolution on the table.

MODERATOR:
A motion has been made to table this resolution. Is there a second? All in favor, please raise your placards. That is ten. Now the opposition. It failed. Are there any other motions? Yes, Senator, move the previous question. All in favor of the previous question, please raise your placards high. Fails. Are there any other motions? We are ready for a speaker affirming the resolution.

SENATOR #15:
Yes, Sir. Alright, Senators, first of all, I would like to speak on something that has not been touched on at this point. Now, currently, Japanese officials use what is called a dock layover. If some kind of vegetable or meat product or other kind of edible food is brought in and they don't feel that they want it, they perhaps will leave it there for five to six weeks and let it sit there and rot. Now while doing this seems to be fair because they have to take time to situate it and make sure it is acceptable, it sits there and rots and American producers lose money.

Now, Senators, what we need to do is and what we need to look at is the protection of our individuals, look at the protection of our producers, which we were quoted by Japanese officials as saying in *U.S. News and World Report*, we protect producers while Americans protect consumers. Japanese are concerned with protecting their producers and we are in turn concerned with helping consumers. Now, Senators, in order to establish ourselves as more of a world power once again, we need to make sure we protect both our consumers and our producers. Now, if we do not protect our farmers we are going to lose an exceedingly large amount of money.

It was brought up, by I believe Senator #14 and various other senators, that we have been viewed as being extremely lazy. I would like you to look at a farmer in the Midwest and go to his farm one day on a hot Saturday afternoon after a long day of labor and look him square in the eye and say, Sir, you are lazy! Where he is cutting everything in order to make very little for his family to live on because of the recession. Now, Senators, this doesn't make sense. According to one report, our trade deficit with Japan was up to approximately sixty million dollars in 1988, and it is dropping at an incredible rate. Now, if that's happening, why is the recession getting worse? Senators, we need to work more on this as a problem and we need to have some kind of establishment where we can reduce the deficit more and more quickly to help our producers and our consumers if that is what is at stake here.

Now, I would like to respond to something stated by Senator #13—that in turn while the Japanese help their producers, we need to help ours. While there are approximately multiple billions of dollars being invested by Japanese government officials in Japanese corporations, they're being called stock reimbursements, or trade loss reimbursements, and the figures are staggering. Now, Senators, if they help their corporations that much, is it so much to ask that we help our producers in our nation, because what we need to think here is not only world economy but domestic economy. We need to do everything we can to help our producers and our consumers in this great nation or we will never get out of the rut we are in. Thank you.

MODERATOR:
Thank you.

SENATOR #18:
Senator, if Japanese industries are so heavily subsidized as you say, how come we have no countervailing duties against the Japanese?

SENATOR #15:
Senators, I can't really respond to that because we have so many different diverse dealings with goods—whereas they are centered around manufactured goods we are more centered around agrarian goods.

MODERATOR:
Questions?

SENATOR #19:
Is the Senator aware that the current recession in the United States is not due to a trade deficit with Japan, but the fact that the trillion dollar debt of the American government does not allow the government to increase governmental spending to promote a recovery?

SENATOR #15:
Well, Senator, I disagree with part of what you said because I think there are various contributors to the federal deficit not being looked at quite as carefully, and I think that if you were to examine two separate areas it would actually contribute to a better whole than just looking at one thing and saying this is the problem. I think it's everything and I think the trade deficit is a large factor.

MODERATOR:
Thank you, Senator. Hearing no motions, we are in line for a negative speaker.

SENATOR #20:

Ever since Senator #13 stole my joke I have been trying to think of another thing to discuss in regard to Japanese policies, and then I started to think about government solutions to another problem which we have had, such as the long lines at the post office. The postmaster general has recently announced that he's working to shorten lines at post offices around the country. From now on when we go to the post office we will have to stand closer together. In other words, it is very difficult for the federal government sometimes to find solutions to our problems. This is nothing but a blanket attempt at a quick-fix solution to one of the serious problems that is facing our country, and that is our own economic weakness. However, the only thing that will come out of this piece of legislation would be an increase of tensions between the United States and Japan.

I think there is one thing that has been largely ignored today when we have been debating this piece of legislation, and that is that to a great degree this legislation will do nothing! Just look at the wording of the actual whereas clauses—it says that the United States will enact the same trade restrictions against Japan that they have closed to us. In other words, we will not buy rice from Japan—we will not buy certain products from Japan that they do not buy from us. That does nothing—the Japanese are not willing to sell rice when they are importing rice. We are enacting the exact same laws that they have. That makes no sense when you think about it. We are trading with them, we are trying to sell them things, why would they try to sell the same things to us? That makes absolutely no sense. The only thing that will happen is that the Japanese will become even more perturbed, and the result of that is that it's highly likely that the Japanese will move their investment to other countries.

The *Far Eastern Economic Review* pointed out last year that if the Japanese continue to lose confidence in the American government's willingness to work with them, then a great deal of Japanese money will leave this country. Now some people have said that's a good thing, but ask yourself this question. If the Japanese remove their money from the American economy, then what will happen? The fact is, the United States companies need the money to reinvest in their companies and as a result of this resolution then American companies will not be able to invest that money in new areas. The more money that comes into the United States economy from other countries, the better, and in reality all this will do is to continue to damage the United States Congress.

Former president Richard Nixon pointed out that if the United States continues to distance itself from the Japanese as well as the Europeans, the recession that we recently had will appear as only a minor blip in comparison to the depression we will have as a result of trade wars. This sets a very dangerous precedent and remember, two wrongs don't make a right—free trade should be the way to go.

MODERATOR:
Questions?

SENATOR #21:
Can they survive without the United States, since we are 75% of their market?

SENATOR #20:
They will be less willing to invest in the United States and that is very important to us.

SENATOR #21:
Isn't it true that this resolution sets up these restrictions only if Japan does not open its markets?

SENATOR #20:
Yes, but that kind of ultimatum will not solve the problem.

MODERATOR:
Thank you. Are there any motions? Yes, Senator? There is a motion to lay the bill on the table. Is there a second? All in favor, please raise your placards. Those opposed? This motion has been laid upon the table.

The Super Session recessed at this time before returning to take up other bills and resolutions.

An Argument Model

An argument consists of three indispensable parts: a *claim*, which the arguer wants the audience to accept; *evidence* offered as support for the claim; and an *inference*, which links the evidence to the claim.

In this text we will use a simplified version of an argument model made popular by Ehninger and Brockriede in *Decision by Debate*.[1] This structural model of reasoning, based on Stephen Toulmin's *The Uses of*

Argument,[2] allows students to visualize the relationship between the three component parts of an argument: evidence, claim, and inference.

Evidence is the information or data provided to secure the acceptance of the claim. Evidence is often referred to as the raw material of proof, or the foundation on which the proof rests. To serve as evidence of a claim, the information or data must be accepted by the audience. The claim is the statement the advocate of the argument wants the audience to accept. The inference involves a mental operation, often supplied by the audience, that links the evidence to the claim. The inference functions to bridge what is known and accepted to that which is unknown or unaccepted.

An example taken from the debate on ''A Resolution Concerning Japanese Trade'' will illustrate how the three components work together in an argument. In this debate Senator #1 claims that Japanese trade practices result in a significant balance-of-trade deficit. To support his position he provides evidence from *The New York Times* that the United States allows unlimited numbers of Japanese autos to be sold in our markets while we are locked out of Japanese markets.

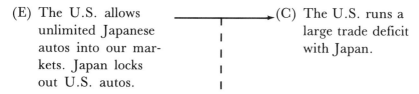

An audience will accept the claim if they believe the evidence to be accurate and if they understand the causal link provided by the inference. In subsequent sections of this chapter, we shall discuss the three essential components of an argument: claims, evidence, and inference.

Claims

A claim is an assertion that the arguer wants accepted. Some of the claims contained in the debate on "A Resolution Concerning Japanese Trade" are as follows:

- Congress should implement the same trade restrictions against Japan that Japan imposes on the United States.
- Japan engages in unfair trade* restrictions against the United States.
- Protectionism is bad economic policy.
- Japanese trade policies harm the United States economy.

Observe that none of these claims is stated explicitly in "A Resolution Concerning Japanese Trade." These claims had to be discovered by analyzing the resolution. Elsewhere in this text we discuss "brainstorming," preliminary research, and "stock issues" analysis as means for determining the actual issues for debate. Douglas Ehninger and Wayne Brockriede remind us that issues are not invented by debaters; they are inherent in the controversy. "Instead of being invented, they are discovered by examining all of the stored-up matters of fact or principle. . . ."[3]

Each of the claims stated above has been written as an affirmative declarative sentence in order that the grounds for debate between the arguments for and against the resolution can be understood. Carefully worded claims that place the burden for change on the advocates of the resolution are necessary for meaningful clash on the issues.

A careful examination of the claims listed above also reveals that each one is different. The first is a policy claim—a call for some action to be taken to resolve a problem. Since bills or resolutions presented for Student Congress debate almost always call for some action to be taken, this will be the *ultimate claim* to be decided by debate. The next three claims are subclaims of meaning, value, and fact. Whether or not the action called for in a bill or resolution is warranted will be determined by the debate on these subclaims.

Claims of *policy* call for a specific course of action to remedy existing problems or to gain benefits not available without the proposed action. Gerald Miller argues that policy claims have no distinguishing characteristics which set them apart from claims of fact and value.[4] The action

---

*This claim could be a claim of fact or a claim of meaning. If unfair trade is ambiguous, a clear definition needs to be established.

called for cannot be justified without appeals to claims of fact or value. To justify the action called for in "A Resolution Concerning Japanese Trade," a debater would have to have a preponderance of evidence and arguments justifying the subclaims. Failure to support the subclaims would logically argue against the proposed action.

Claims of *meaning* may or may not be discovered when a bill or resolution is being evaluated for debate. If key terms in a bill or resolution are ambiguous, some definition or interpretation of these terms will be necessary for debate to proceed. If, for example, "unfair trade" means one thing to those who favor the resolution and something different to those who oppose the resolution, the debate will be muddled and progress toward a solution to the problem will be difficult. If those in favor of the resolution consider fair trade to be a system of mutually agreed upon tariffs and quotas, and those who oppose the resolution believe that fair trade means no tariffs or quotas, debate will not be fruitful. If claims of meaning are discovered, they need to be resolved before other claims are addressed. A more comprehensive discussion of claims of meaning (definition) can be found in *Decision by Debate*.[5]

Claims of *value* are judgmental. These claims attempt to assign some measure of worth to the object of evaluation. When value claims are made it is necessary to develop a conceptual framework that provides some fixed criteria for measuring value. If a debater supports the claim that "protectionism is bad economic policy," some economic criteria need to be established to measure the impact of protectionist actions. If the arguments presented to support the claim indicate that protectionist trade policies result in additional barriers to trade, in reduced exports, in lost markets, and in larger balance-of-trade deficits, the debater will have succeeded in demonstrating that such policies are of negative worth. An opponent may well argue that protectionist measures are the only weapons we have against nations that have open access to our markets while effectively locking us out of their markets. The relative economic impact of these conflicting positions will need to be evaluated in order to determine whether protectionism is bad. An excellent discussion of value propositions (claims) can be found in *Critical Thinking and Communication: The Use of Reason in Argument*.[6]

Claims of *fact*, according to Barbara Warnick and Edward Inch, "make inferences about past, present, or future conditions or relationships."[7] Claims of fact that are empirically verifiable are not normally argued. In the first whereas clause of "A Resolution Concerning Japanese Trade," there appears to be an empirical claim of fact: "The

United States has a trade deficit of 185 billion dollars with just Japan.'' If one could assume that the statement means that the past year's deficit was 185 billion dollars, one could conclude that the statement was either true or false. Rather than debate the claim, it would make more sense to take the total dollar value of U.S. exports and the total dollar value of Japanese imports and compute the deficit. A reading of the transcript of the debate makes it abundantly clear that there is no agreement on the size of the deficit.

Warnick and Inch break factual claims into three types: relational claims, predictive claims, and claims of historical fact.[8] ''Japanese trade policies harm the United States economy'' is an example of a relational claim. To support this claim a debater would have to establish a causal relationship between Japanese trade policies and economic harms suffered by the United States.

An example of a predictive claim of fact might be ''Trade deficits with Japan will continue until the U.S. retaliates.'' When arguing a predictive claim one assumes that past conditions serve as a sign of future conditions. Finally, a claim of historical fact, such as ''Japan has always protected its industries against foreign competition,'' might be advanced to support the argument that U.S. action against Japan is necessary. Evidence of past trade policies with other countries would have to be examined to support or deny this claim.

While it is true that many claims of fact are not controversial and are better resolved by empirical means, there are a host of factual claims that are not amenable to immediate verification. Many claims of fact are open to dispute and they play a prominent role in determining whether action called for in policy claims ought to be taken.

Evidence

Evidence consists of data or information provided to gain acceptance of a claim. Not all information functions as evidence. For information to serve as evidence in an argument it must meet two conditions: (1) the information must be believed by the audience, and (2) some principle of reasoning (inference) must connect the evidence to the claim. If the information offered as evidence is not believed by the audience the claim will not be accepted, and if the evidence is not logically connected to the claim then it should not be accepted. The first condition is essentially psychological and the second condition is essentially logical.

Ideally, the logical characteristics of the evidence should enhance its psychological impact. All of us are aware of claims that have been accepted even though the evidence offered is weak, and likewise, we know of claims that have been rejected even though a substantial amount of evidence has been offered to support the claim. When important policy decisions are made that will affect the future, it is vital that we pay close attention to the logical foundation on which the claim rests. If, for example, a favorable vote on "A Resolution Concerning Japanese Trade" turns on cultural animosity without due consideration of all of the evidence offered by both parties to the debate, we may regret the action. Experience teaches us that logical decisions are more reliable and more dependable than emotional decisions.

THE SUBSTANCE OF EVIDENCE

Now that we have defined evidence in terms of its function in an argument, it is time to turn to the broad categories of information that may be offered as evidence. Several argumentation texts[9] describe three categories of information that function as evidence: fact, opinion, and previously established claims. We shall examine each category in turn.

Evidence of fact consists of statements that can be verified. Presumably, anyone with access to the relevant information could determine whether a statement of fact is accurate. Evidence of fact is based either upon our own observations of reality—we tend to believe what we see, hear, smell, taste, or touch—or upon statements of others who testify as to what they have observed. In the debate on "A Resolution Concerning Japanese Trade," the statement that our balance-of-trade deficit is $185 billion is either accurate or inaccurate. A look at the available economic data will confirm or deny the accuracy of the statement. Almost all factual evidence in Student Congress debates will consist of testimony. Only rarely will students debating matters of public policy be in the position to make personal observations that are relevant to the outcome of the debate. Since students will most often utilize the testimony of others to provide the factual foundation for claims they support, it is important that they be able to distinguish between testimony consisting of statements of fact from testimony consisting of statements of opinion. Testimony consisting of statements of fact is recorded observations of others; testimony consisting of statements of opinion is recorded interpretations of the observations of others.

Evidence of opinion consists of statements that offer judgments about reality. As such, these statements cannot be literally true or false in the same sense that a statement of fact is either true or false. While it is possible to verify the size of the balance-of-trade deficit with Japan, it is not possible to verify the statement ''Japan's trade policies are inherently unfair.'' In the first instance, a look at the economic data will confirm or deny the truth of the statement. The locus of disagreement lies ''out there'' in the economic data. In the second instance, the locus of disagreement lies in the attitude that the speaker brings to the debate. The statement ''Japan's trade policies are inherently unfair'' says nothing about the properties of the trade deficit; rather, the statement provides information about the speaker's state of mind. The transcript of the Student Congress debate makes it clear that debaters, looking at the same information or data, can come to nearly opposite opinions concerning the fairness of Japanese trade policies. We often have trouble distinguishing facts from opinions because both are often made known to us through the statements of others. Since evidence provides the foundation for the acceptance or rejection of claims, knowing whether we are dealing with fact or opinion is crucial. Evidence of fact can be verified; evidence of opinion cannot be verified. While both fact and opinion function to induce acceptance or rejection of claims, each is different and each has to be evaluated by different standards. In the next section of this chapter we will consider the appropriate tests.

Previously established claims as evidence. In this chapter, we have said that claims are statements that an arguer wants an audience to accept. To gain acceptance of a claim, evidence that an audience will believe is offered as support. Assuming that the audience accepts the evidence and sees the connection between the evidence and the claim, then the claim is established. Once a claim is accepted it can then serve as evidence for further claims. In Student Congress debates, the final or ultimate claim can be established only by developing subclaims of meaning, fact, and value. A chain of reasoning is involved. Typically, we do not vote for policy proposals until we have been convinced that a significant problem exists, that the cause of the problem has been correctly identified, and that the action called for is going to remedy the problem without causing more serious problems. To get to a vote we move through a chain of inferences until we arrive at a final claim. The evidence for the individual argument in a chain of reasoning is the claim of the preceding argument. The following diagram may assist in making clear how chains of argument proceed:

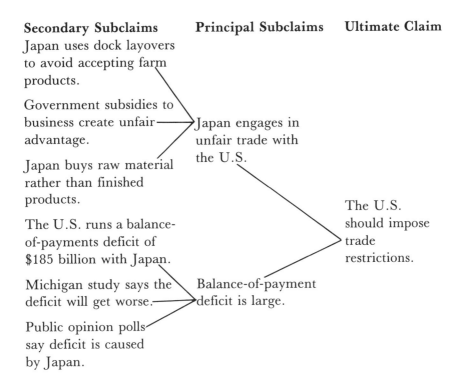

Secondary Subclaims

Japan uses dock layovers to avoid accepting farm products.

Government subsidies to business create unfair advantage.

Japan buys raw material rather than finished products.

The U.S. runs a balance-of-payments deficit of $185 billion with Japan.

Michigan study says the deficit will get worse.

Public opinion polls say deficit is caused by Japan.

Principal Subclaims

Japan engages in unfair trade with the U.S.

Balance-of-payment deficit is large.

Ultimate Claim

The U.S. should impose trade restrictions.

While this is an incomplete layout of arguments that took place in the debate, you can see that claims established are used as evidence for further claims leading up to the ultimate claim in the debate.

TYPES AND TESTS OF EVIDENCE

Argumentation texts classify evidence in many ways. Some texts use as few as three categories, while other texts use as many as seven.[10] We will limit our discussion to the types of evidence that are most often used in legislative debates. Participants in Student Congress debates may on rare occasions offer personal observations to support a claim or may introduce into evidence some artifact; however, the dominant form of evidence is testimony from written sources. Gerald Miller discusses two types of testimony: testimony composed of statistical data and testimony composed of authority-based assertion.[11] Since statistical conclusions are statements about entire populations based on a sampling of those populations, the reliability of these conclusions will be determined by the precision with which the statistical data is collected, by the representativeness of the sample, and by the statistical methods used to treat the data. Testimony composed of authority-based assertion will depend in good measure on who makes the statement. Source credibility is the most important measure of the effectiveness of this form of evidence.

The sample Student Congress debate provides us with a number of examples of evidence composed of statistical data and evidence composed of authority-based assertion. Speaking in favor of the resolution, Senator #1 tells us, "Despite the U.S.'s higher production of cars and the Japanese's lower production, a Michigan study predicts that the deficit will worsen. The automobile trade deficit is predicted to go up to 47%, to 45.7 billion in 1994. How can a country like ours that produces so much fall so far behind? In a poll by *Newsweek* magazine in 1992, 67% of the people surveyed said that unfair trade practices by the Japanese were our reason for being behind in trade." Unfortunately, the source citations are most incomplete and our ability to test the evidence is diminished. If, however, we assume the statistical data to be accurately reported, we need to ask a number of questions about the data before we accept it as evidence that would cause us to take the action against Japan called for in the resolution.

A first question might be, What do the authors of the study consider a Japanese car to be? Do they include Japanese cars that are produced in both the United States and in Japan, or just those produced in Japan? If we do not know precisely what they are measuring, we cannot make an intelligent evaluation of the evidence. We should also question the accuracy of a prediction that is at least two years into the future, given the volatile nature of the global economy. Finally, we could ask how important the trade difference is in automobiles. The balance-of-trade deficit is made up of all items of trade between the two nations and it may be more important for the United States to lessen the trade deficit by concentrating on increasing our export of goods and services other than automobiles. The second piece of statistical data reports the findings of a public-opinion poll. Even if we assume that the poll was fairly conducted and the data properly analyzed, we need to recognize that a public-opinion poll is evidence of what people believe to be true, not necessarily what is true. What we believe to be true and what is actually true may be substantially different.

A second instance of the use of testimony composed of statistical data is offered by Senator #11 to disprove the argument that Japan has closed its markets to U.S. business and that its practices are unfair. Senator

#11 cites a December 30 issue of *National Review*: ''Japan is the second largest importer of American goods with 49 billion dollars a year they're injecting into our economy. The Japanese spend $395 per person on American goods, while Americans only spend $359 per person on Japanese goods. Japan devoted 1.7% of its gross national product to American goods and we devoted only 1.6% of ours to Japanese goods. Moreover, Japan's trade surplus has dropped 27% since its peak in 1987, while American exports to Japan have increased more than to any other nation in the world.'' Citing a March 2, 1992, issue of *U.S. News and World Report*, Senator #11 continues: ''Japan's tariff for industrial products is 2.6%. America's, in case anyone is curious, is 3%, and according to the World Bank, Japan's non-tariff barriers such as quotas and licenses are comparable to America's.''

Among questions to be asked about these statistical data are the following:

- Since the population of the United States is much larger than that of Japan and since the gross national product of the United States is dramatically larger than that of Japan, do the percentages cited mean that Japan is not engaging in unfair trade?

- Does the fact that the trade deficit is not as large now as in 1987 mean that the deficit is insignificant?

- Can these similar percentages be the result of large subsidies provided by the Japanese government to Japanese businesses?

- Can you use quantitative data to establish a qualitative argument, namely, that Japan does not engage in unfair trade practices?

- Does Japan use means other than tariffs, quotas, or licensing to keep U.S. goods out of its market?

Since both sides in the debate use testimony composed of statistical data to persuade members of the Senate, it is necessary that this data be tested rigorously.

The sample debate is replete with examples of testimony composed of authority-based assertions. Senator #7 cites an economist, Alan S. Blinder, writing in *Business Week*, as saying: ''There are three myths. No. 1—Trade deficits do not cause unemployment. No. 2—Our trade deficit has almost gone away. And No. 3—Our trade problems are not made in Japan.'' Since all testimony composed of authority-based assertions depends on the credibility of the source, it is important to ask:

Is Alan S. Blinder an expert in the area of trade relations? Does he have access to all of the relevant data necessary to come to the conclusions he makes? Does he have a track record of being a reliable economist? Does he have a vested interest in the outcome of the debate on trade policy? Do other economists support his conclusions? If economists are divided on these issues, where does the preponderance of expert opinion reside? Finally, one would also want to ask questions about *Business Week*, the source of Blinder's remarks. Publications, as well as individuals, develop reputations that need to be considered when evaluating evidence. Does *Business Week* favor one trade policy over another, or does it provide a balanced account of competing views? Is the publication essentially liberal or conservative? Does the editorial policy of the magazine favor the policies of one political party? Is its policy pro-business or pro-consumer or neither? Answers to these questions need to be considered when testing the evidence used to support claims. Claims are no stronger than the evidence on which they rest. If we are to make critical decisions that will stand the test of informed scrutiny, we must pay careful attention to the evidence submitted.

It has been our experience that most evidence used by students engaged in legislative debate will consist of testimony. This does not imply that there are no other types of evidence or that other types of evidence are unimportant. A number of argumentation texts provide general guidelines for testing a whole array of evidence. A reasonably complete list of guidelines can be found in *Critical Thinking and Communication: The Use of Reason in Argument*.[12] Warnick and Inch suggest that evidence be tested under the following general criteria: reliability, expertise, objectivity, consistency, recency, relevance, access, and accuracy of citation.

Inference

An *inference* functions to link evidence to claims—it involves a mental operation in which an individual infers the truth or falsity of one statement (claim) given the truth or falsity of another statement (evidence). A comprehensive treatment of inferences, which would include a discussion of syllogisms and the rules of formal validity, is well beyond the scope of this text. We have consciously avoided a treatment of syllogistic reasoning and the rules of formal validity for two reasons. While one may establish formal validity in a hypothetical universe in which all the necessary conditions are satisfied, the system breaks down if used as a model for practical reasoning. Secondly, the ultimate claim in any policy debate that makes predictions about the future will necessarily be a probability statement. We cannot be certain that new policies will work precisely as predicted. Standards imposed by the rules of formal validity require that claims follow from evidence with absolute certainty. Attempts to adapt syllogistic reasoning to the realm of the probable are exceedingly difficult. This decision to avoid a discussion of syllogistic reasoning and formal validity is not intended to imply that they are unimportant.

This section of the chapter will focus on several of the most common types of inferences that the mind makes when relating evidence to the acceptance of claims. Inferences have been made by students since early childhood. Our goal in this chapter is to have students understand the inferential process. This includes the ability to give names to the various forms that inferences take, understand how they operate, and apply appropriate tests of reasoning to determine whether the mental leap is justified.

Before turning to specific types of inference, it is important to remember that the ultimate claim in a policy debate is a probability statement. The claim of the argument goes beyond the evidence presented. No one can be certain that the actions advocated by supporters of "A Resolution Concerning Japanese Trade" will in fact cause Japan to change its trade policies in ways that will benefit the United States. People will accept the proposed actions against Japan if they are convinced that there is a strong probability that the action will be beneficial; they will reject the proposal if they think it will be too risky. Since the ultimate claim of a policy proposal can never be certain, we need a standard other than that of formal validity to apply to claims that go beyond the evidence.

Patterson and Zarefsky propose a "standard of reasonableness" that they argue is more demanding than logical possibility but less demanding than formal validity. They argue that "experience, rather than abstract logic, decides which inferences people will judge to be sound . . . Generally, an inference is reasonable if (1) the underlying assumptions of the argument are shared by the audience and (2) the form of the inference is correct. The first condition is *substantive*, as it relates to the content of the argument, and the second condition is *formal*, as it relates to the argument's structure."[13] In the debate on "A Resolution Concerning Japanese Trade," those who favor the resolution argue that Japan engages in unfair trade with the United States. They present evidence that the Japanese government provides subsidies to Japanese industries that allow them to offer products on the market below actual costs, that the Japanese government utilizes dock layovers to discourage U.S. export of agricultural products to Japan, and that the Japanese government mandates unrealistic automobile standards to keep American automobiles out of Japan. If the senators in the chamber share the underlying assumption that trade between countries should be governed by rules that are fair to both, the inference will seem reasonable.

Every debate that takes place does so in a context of basic assumptions that are widely accepted. Inferences that conflict with these basic assumptions will likely be rejected. It would, of course, be impossible to account for all the assumptions underlying the wide array of controversial topics. What we do know is that underlying assumptions are content-specific and that there is no substitute for being well informed on the topic being debated.

The second condition for reasonableness depends on the acceptance of the form the inference takes in an argument. All of us use a variety of inferences each day, and experience teaches us which forms of inference produce acceptable claims. While it may be true that a person may intuit good arguments and argue reasonably well, we think that students will become more proficient users and critics of arguments if they learn to identify the most commonly used inferences. The purpose of learning to apply labels is to help us perceive differences. Our understanding of the inferential process is likely to be vague and imprecise if we cannot distinguish between the various forms of inference. The ability to label inferences, however, is not sufficient. Students must also understand the mental process involved and be able to test the inference to determine its acceptability. Argumentation texts vary widely in the treatment of inferences but most consider, in one way or another, five common forms: example/generalization, analogy, sign, cause, and authority. The remainder of this chapter will be devoted to a discussion of these common forms of inference.

INFERENCES FROM EXAMPLE/GENERALIZATION

Inferences from example/generalization rest on the notion that what is true of specific members of a class will also be true of other members of the class or of the class as a whole. Whether one moves from specific instances to a general claim or from a generalization to a claim about a specific instance, the inference is the same. Inferences based on example are used in two types of arguments. Statistical generalizations are based on sample populations that are purported to be a microcosm of the total population. Public-opinion polls frequently sample as few as a thousand voters in a state to arrive at reasonably accurate statistical generalizations about all voters in that state. In our sample debate, the statement from *Newsweek* that 67% of the public believes our trade deficit with Japan is the result of unfair trade practices is a statistical generalization. There is no guarantee that the statement is reliable just because it contains quantitative data. Before accepting any statistical generalization a number of tests need to be applied. Common tests include the following:

1. Are the units represented by the statistics clearly defined?

2. Is the sample large enough to support the generalization?

3. Is the sample representative of the population from which it is drawn?

If we apply these tests to the example from *Newsweek* cited above, we would ask what it means to say that 67% of the ''public'' believes that Japan engages in unfair trade. Does the public include all citizens of the United States, all adults, only adults engaged in commerce? Unless we know what is being measured, the statement is not very meaningful. Secondly, if the survey conducted by *Newsweek* was limited to only a handful of people, we could conclude that the generalization was not warranted. Likewise, if the survey was conducted by phone to residential customers during the day, we would have reason to question the representativeness of the sample. This sampling would not include most of the people in the work force.

A second form of inference from example is by enumeration. An arguer identifies several examples and then draws a general conclusion from these examples. In our sample debate, Senator #11 uses two examples to support the claim that protectionist trade policies can only hurt the United States. He tells us that the Smoot-Hawley Tariff Act that established higher tariffs resulted in retaliation and lower world trade, and that while restrictions on Japanese steel imports saved 17,000 U.S. jobs in the steel market, this action cost us 54,000 jobs in other markets. If the audience accepts these two examples as protectionist measures, they may well conclude that protectionist measures are counterproductive. Four tests can be applied:

1. Are enough examples provided to justify the generalization?

2. Are the examples relevant?

3. Are the examples typical or representative?

4. If counterexamples exist, can they be shown to be unimportant?

If we apply these tests to the argument of Senator #11, we would have to determine if his two examples are sufficient to justify the claim that protectionist measures are harmful. As a rule of thumb, the more examples one can provide the stronger the inference. However, there is no magic number of examples to determine whether we should accept the claim or not. It may well be the case that Senator #11 has many examples that justify his claim, but time constraints and the patience of the audience are important considerations in his decision to limit his presentation to two examples. If these are the only two instances in the history of trade relations, then we can conclude that his generalization is extremely weak. We have to search for answers in the context of the controversy itself to determine whether these two examples are sufficient.

The test of relevance has to do with determining whether or not the two examples are instances of protectionism. If they are, then the examples belong to the same class of actions about which the claim is made and the claim meets the test of relevance; if not, the claim should be rejected. To be typical or representative, the two examples should exhibit most of the characteristics of protectionism. If the examples have not been fairly selected from instances of actions by the United States to protect its markets, then we can conclude that the examples are atypical and do not justify the claim being made. Finally, we know from experience that one good counterexample can undermine a claim based on an enumeration of examples. To be successful a debater who uses examples to arrive at a generalization must be able to explain why a counterexample does not diminish the claim. For example, if an opponent argued that the United States protects its nuclear-weapons industry and that there have been no adverse reactions to this policy, Senator #11 could argue that this negative example is not relevant. There is no open market for nuclear weapons.

Inference from generalization is a third type of argument. As we stated earlier, the inferential process is the same as that employed in inferences from example. The process is just reversed and we move from a generalization (evidence) to a specific example (claim). If the history of trade relations between the U.S. and Japan revealed that each restrictive trade measure imposed by the U.S. was countered by an equally restrictive Japanese measure, a debater could argue that the Japanese government will retaliate if the resolution passes. This argument could be diagramed as follows:

(E) Japan will retaliate if ————————▸(C) For example, Japan
the resolution passes.   will no longer make
                                      capital investments in
                                      the U.S.
(I) Japan has consistently
countered U.S. trade
restrictions.

The inference is that the specific example in the claim is representative of the class of actions described in the evidence. The tests to be applied are the same as those for claims derived by enumeration.

INFERENCES FROM ANALOGY

While it is not uncommon for argumentation texts to refer to inference from analogy as logically less rigorous than other forms of inference, most of these texts indicate that it is nevertheless one of the most important means of arguing. The reason is that most of our early learning occurs by means of analogy. All analogies involve some kind of comparison. Jack Ray and Harry Zavos tell us that "comparison is basic to observation. The act of perception is an act of making comparisons, of judging sameness and difference. Furthermore, the act of labeling in language depends upon comparisons. Literal and figurative comparisons or metaphors are basic to language and thought."[14] Because analogies compare what is unknown to what is familiar, and because comparison is fundamental to early learning and language acquisition, analogies tend to be very effective.

The terms *literal* and *figurative* are often used to describe two types of analogies—literal analogies are comparisons of two ideas or things of the same class, and figurative analogies are comparisons of two ideas or things of different classes. If one observes that the United States has a strong heavy-industry base, a strong high-tech base, strong capital markets, and a strong agricultural base that make the country an economic superpower, and the audience knows that Japan is an economic superpower with a strong heavy-industry base, a strong high-tech base, and strong capital markets, listeners might conclude that Japan probably has a strong agricultural base as well. The evidence in this literal analogy consists of the statements about both the United States and Japan that are known; the claim draws the conclusion that Japan will probably have a strong agricultural base. The inference, implicit in the argument, is that Japan is similar to the United States in all important respects that affect the claim. To determine the strength of literal analogies, we must determine whether essential similarities outweigh essential differences. We must ask if there are important differences between the United States and Japan. Since Japan is only about the size of California, and since Japan's population is approximately one-half that of the United States, it is clear that Japan does not have the land mass to produce significant agricultural products. The second test to apply asks whether the differences between the two objects being compared are significant. This argument is a very weak analogy because there are important differences between the United States and Japan and the differences are crucial to the claim being made. The argument could be diagramed as follows:

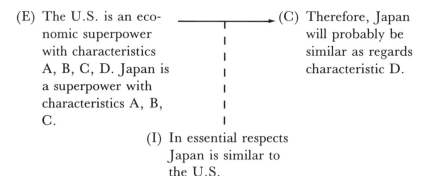

(E) The U.S. is an economic superpower with characteristics A, B, C, D. Japan is a superpower with characteristics A, B, C.

(C) Therefore, Japan will probably be similar as regards characteristic D.

(I) In essential respects Japan is similar to the U.S.

While literal analogies make direct comparisons, figurative analogies make indirect comparisons. In our sample debate, Senator #11 claims that Japan will take advantage of the United States if the resolution passes. He argues that "cows do indeed practice protectionist policies. Whenever there is the slightest hint of danger a group of cows will huddle in a circle to prevent anyone else from getting in. Yet, despite this we . . . continue to milk cows for all they're worth. If the United States establishes such a protectionist policy, Japan will continue to milk us for all we're worth." The point of this argument is that just as cows are vulnerable despite practicing protectionist measures, so the United States will be even if we practice protectionist measures. There is not much that we can say about such inferences in figurative analogies except that they are "intuitive" and that they can be useful. If they illuminate an important concept they can be very persuasive.

INFERENCES FROM SIGN

Everyone uses inferences from sign. When we approach a traffic signal and the light turns red it is a sign that we should stop. When we have stomach cramps it is a sign that we are ill. Statistical data that the unemployment rate is increasing is a sign that we are having economic problems. When the president calls the National Security Council into a late-night meeting, it is a sign that something important requires immediate attention. We use clues or symptoms that we can observe to infer conditions that we cannot observe.

The sample NFL Student Congress debate that we have used as a reference for discussing arguments took place in June 1992. The campaign for the presidency of the United States was well under way at that time. The dominant issue in the campaign was the state of the economy. In this context Senator #14 argues that the attacks on Japan by the Bush administration are motivated not by trade imbalances but by the need for President Bush to be reelected. If we diagramed this argument it would appear as follows:

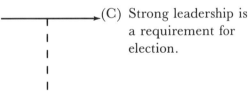

(E) The Bush administration is aggressively attacking Japanese trade policies. ⟶ (C) Strong leadership is a requirement for election.

(I) Aggressive policies are a sign of strong leadership.

We can handle sign inferences without worrying about causation. It is enough to know that in the past signs and events were associated in such a way that when the sign is present we can expect the event with a certain probability. To test inferences from sign we ask if an alternative explanation of the relationship is more likely. If so we do not have a reliable sign inference. Conventional wisdom tells us that if there are several signs pointing to the same condition, the inference will be stronger. Finally, a debater will need to be able to account for any contrary signs.

INFERENCES FROM CAUSE

The notion of causation is very complicated. We use inferences from cause to account for changes that we observe in the natural world, to assign responsibility for actions that result in favorable or unfavorable outcomes, and to make predictions about future actions. Although it may be easy to comprehend the statement "Drinking a fifth of gin on an empty stomach will cause drunkenness," it is not easy to establish that the actions called for in "A Resolution Concerning Japanese Trade" will cause Japan to alter its trade policies to benefit the United States. Arguments involving inferences from cause will figure prominently in Student Congress debates. It is not reasonable to call for future action to be taken unless there are significant problems that can be solved by the proposed action or unless benefits can only be obtained by the course of action called for in a bill or resolution. If debaters are not able to identify the cause of existing problems, the solution they propose may only treat symptoms of the problem. Treating symptoms will not suffice; as long as the causes of the problem remain, the problem will persist. It is likewise necessary for debaters to offer convincing evidence that action taken to derive future benefits will, in fact, be generated by the action. If they cannot establish the causal relationship between the prescribed action and the benefits claimed, then the bill or resolution should be rejected. All arguments that call for future action involve risk, and intelligent people do not take risks unless there is a strong probability that the action called for will be beneficial.

To justify the action called for in the ultimate claim in the debate on "A Resolution Concerning Japanese Trade," it is necessary that the proponents of the resolution prove that the unfair trade practices of the Japanese government are the primary cause of our balance-of-trade deficit. They must also prove that the sanctions advocated will be sufficient to cause the Japanese to drop these unfair practices. If Japanese trade policies are not the cause of our balance-of-trade deficit, then changing those policies will not solve our problem. Even if the proponents of the resolution succeed in proving that Japanese trade policies are the primary cause of our deficit, they cannot justify the resolution unless they can also prove that the actions advocated will cause the Japanese to change their unfair policies. A layout of one of the above arguments will help us visualize the mental operation involved in inferences from cause.

(E) Quotas, tariffs, li-   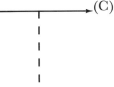   (C) The U.S. balance-
censing procedures,   of-trade deficit with
and dock layovers   Japan is significant
are used by Japan to   and harmful.
keep U.S. goods out
of its markets.

(I) Policies that unfairly
restrict exports cause
trade imbalances.

Causal inferences are subject to several tests. First, is the cause cited capable of producing the effect made in the claim? If Japan erects trade barriers to keep most U.S. products out of its markets and the United States allows Japan largely unrestricted access to our markets, then the inference is reasonable. The fact that trade barriers can cause a balance-of-trade-deficit, however, does not necessarily mean that the barriers cited in the evidence did in fact cause the trade deficit. Secondly, we need to ask if there are other causes that better account for the trade deficit. In our sample Student Congress debate, much of the deficit is attributed to an imbalance of trade in the automobile industry. If the reason American cars are not purchased in Japan is that they are inferior products and are designed for driving on the right side of the road rather than the left, then the causal inference in our example is unreasonable.

Claims derived from causal inferences vary widely in their reliability. We always need to be aware of multiple causes, alternative causes, intervening causes, and counteracting causes that may affect the force of the claim. The United States' balance-of-trade deficit is most likely the result of multiple causes at work. The deficit could be caused by trade agreements negotiated under GATT, bilateral trade agreements between the U.S. and Japan, differences in consumer demand in both the U.S. and Japan, and the unwillingness of American businesses to invest in Japan. When complex policy arguments are advanced, inferences from cause are rarely simple and straightforward.

INFERENCES FROM AUTHORITY

Earlier in this chapter we argued that debaters rely heavily on testimony to prove their arguments. The rapid advances in technology, the increasing complexity of the world in which we live, and the explosion of information available make it difficult for anyone to speak with authority on a large number of current issues. When we use inferences from authority we assert that the claim is reasonable because the statement comes from a reliable source. If the audience believes the source to be credible, it will accept the claim of the argument; if not, it will reject the claim. The evidence in an argument from authority consists of a statement of fact or opinion along with an identification of the source. The claim in the argument is a restatement of the evidence by the speaker, and the inference says you should believe the claim because the source is credible. Examine the layout of the following argument by Senator #11:

(E) According to the economist Henry George, what protectionism teaches us to do to ourselves at peace is what our enemies seek to do to us in times of war.

(C) Keeping other countries out of our markets keeps our economy from working the way it should.

(I) What economist George says about trade policy is worthy of belief.

If your audience does not know who Henry George is, calling him an economist may not suffice. A source's credibility can be enhanced by providing the audience with his qualifications. Senator #11 seeks to do this when he cites Paul Samuelson. Reference is made to Samuelson's academic background and his position on the Council of Economic Advisers during the Reagan administration.

The form of inference from authority is simple: "The claim is true because authority X made the statement." We encounter difficulties, however, when various sources speak authoritatively on different sides of controversial issues. Several senators in our sample debate cite authoritative sources to prove that our balance-of-trade-deficit is caused by Japanese trade policies, while other senators cite authoritative sources to prove that this is not true. Whom do we trust? A number of tests have been designed to assist us in making informed decisions.

First, we ask whether the source is qualified by training and experience to speak on the issue. Economist Paul Samuelson is certainly well known. He is frequently asked to testify before congressional committees, to advise government agencies on economic policy, and to serve on important government councils. His economics book is a standard text for many college and university courses, and he has a reputation for making good decisions.

A second question that we ask is whether the source has access to all the relevant information necessary to make informed statements about the issue being debated. Training and experience are necessary, but without firsthand information on the issue being debated, the expert opinion should be discounted.

Next, we should ask if the source is reasonably unbiased. If a source has a vested interest in the outcome of a debate, the source may well slant the argument. An economist on the payroll of a political party who supports the economic agenda of that party should have his or her statements scrutinized very carefully.

A fourth check on inferences from authority can be made by determining if the testimony is consistent with other sources of information. Multiple sources of information that point to the same conclusion increase the likelihood that the testimony is worthy of belief. When faced with conflicting testimony on an issue, we should ask where the consensus lies.

Finally, we should ask if the testimony used in a debate accurately represents the views of the source. While it may be accurate to say that as a general principle Paul Samuelson strongly supports free trade and thinks that protectionist trade policies are usually ill advised, it may be inaccurate to use a theory statement of his unless the context of his statement is directly relevant to the debate on "A Resolution Concerning Japanese Trade." It is certainly possible that Paul Samuelson might argue that there are instances where trade imbalances are so severe that sanctions are necessary to bring about open markets. Debaters are obligated to use statements of authorities that accurately reflect their thinking as it relates to the issue being debated.

Summary

An understanding of how arguments function in a legislative setting is crucial to successful advocacy for Student Congress participants. To this end we have limited our discussion of argumentation theory to public-policy debates that call for action to be voted upon by members of a legislative body. We have included practical information that we think will be useful to student participants. The transcript of an NFL Student Congress debate in this chapter serves two purposes: it is a "model" debate that includes several different types of arguments for students to examine, and the debate provides useful examples for our discussion of arguments.

A simplified version of Toulmin's model of argument is included to help students visualize the relationship between the components of an argument: claim, evidence, and inference. The claim is an assertion that an arguer wants the audience to accept; it provides the basis for controversy. Evidence consists of any information or data that an audience will accept as support for the claim; evidence is the factual foundation on which the claim rests. Inferences are mental operations we employ to link the evidence to the claim.

In this chapter we discussed claims of policy, claims of meaning, claims of fact, and claims of value. Since Student Congress bills or resolutions call for some action to be taken, the final claim to be established will be a policy claim. Policy claims express dissatisfaction with existing policy or advocate new policy to derive benefits. Since policy claims make predictions about the future, they can never be certain. Claims of meaning are necessary when key terms are ambiguous. Before debates can proceed to resolution, both parties to the dispute must have a common understanding of these terms.

Claims of value make judgments about the worth of objects being evaluated. If one claims that a policy of "fair trade" is more desirable than a policy of "free trade," we would expect that person to provide criteria or standards for making this judgment. Claims of fact make inferences about past, present, or future conditions or relationships. "Japan has always opposed free trade policies" is a claim of past fact; "Japan is currently engaging in unfair trade policies" is a claim of present fact; "Japan will retaliate if the U.S. imposes trade sanctions" is a claim of future fact. The ability to identify the kind of claim that we make or that other persons make is important. Proof requirements differ for different kinds of claims.

Evidence is provided to gain support for a claim. For information to serve as evidence it must be linked to the claim by some form of reasoning, and it must be believed by the audience. Three categories of information function as evidence: fact, opinion, and previously established claims. Evidence of fact consists of statements that can be verified. Evidence of opinion consists of statements that interpret what has been observed and makes judgments about the observation. Previously established claims serve as evidence in chains of argument. The predominant types of evidence used in Student Congress debates are testimony composed of statistical data and testimony composed of authority-based assertion. The ability to identify types of evidence and to apply the appropriate tests of evidence will make it possible for students to develop good arguments and evaluate the arguments of others.

An inference involves a mental operation that links evidence to a claim. While inferences can never be certain, they can be reasonable. Audiences will consider inferences reasonable if they understand and share the underlying assumptions of the argument and if they can visualize the relationship of the evidence to the claim. We limited our discussion of inferences to five common forms: example/generalization, analogy, sign, cause, and authority. Inferences from example/generalization relate parts to wholes and wholes to parts; inferences from analogy involve comparisons—literal analogies compare objects from the same class and figurative analogies involve comparisons of objects from different classes; inferences from sign use clues or symptoms that we can observe to infer conditions that we cannot observe; inferences from cause account for the influence of one event or object on another event or object; and inferences from authority rest on the judgment of experts.

Notes

1. Douglas Ehninger and Wayne Brockriede, *Decision by Debate* (New York: Dodd, Mead, 1968), 98–109.

2. Stephen Toulmin, *The Uses of Argument* (Cambridge: Cambridge University Press, 1969).

3. Ehninger and Brockriede, 92.

4. Gerald R. Miller, "Evidence and Argument," in Gerald R. Miller and Thomas R. Nilsen, eds., *Perspectives on Argumentation* (Chicago: Scott, Foresman, 1966), 36.

5. Ehninger and Brockriede, 102.

6. Barbara Warnick and Edward S. Inch, *Critical Thinking and Communication: The Use of Reason in Argument* (New York: Macmillan, 1989), 187–216.

7. Warnick and Inch, 57.

8. Warnick and Inch, 57–58.

9. Ehninger and Brockriede, and Warnick and Inch.

10. Warnick and Inch cite three and Ehninger and Brockriede cite seven.

11. Miller, 37–47.

12. Warnick and Inch, 71–77.

13. J. W. Patterson and David Zarefsky, *Contemporary Debate* (Boston: Houghton Mifflin, 1983), 42–46.

14. Jack Ray and Harry Zavos, "Reasoning and Argument: Some Special Problems and Types," in Gerald R. Miller and Thomas R. Nilsen, *Perspectives on Argumentation* (Chicago: Scott, Foresman, 1966), 96–98.

Discussion Questions

1. How would a weakness in evidence or inference undermine the argument of which it is a part?

2. Under what conditions might people choose to settle their differences by means other than arguments?

3. How do the four types of claims—meaning, fact, value, and policy—differ?

4. What are the merits of supporting a claim with different types of evidence as opposed to relying on one type of evidence?

5. Is evidence that is derived from experimental studies subject to bias? Why or why not?

6. How do you distinguish between an inference from sign and an inference from cause?

7. Discuss the following statement: Inferences from analogy are logically weak.

8. Why are bills and resolutions written to favor change?

9. Why must contemporary men and women make many decisions on the basis of authority?

10. Why should all citizens in a democracy be able to engage in the give-and-take of argument?

11. In what sense is an issue vital to the life of the ultimate claim?

12. What conditions must be met before information functions as evidence?

13. How can statistical evidence be verified?

14. When terms in a bill or resolution are defined, why should they be defined within the context of the controversy?

CHAPTER 2

Responding to Arguments

In Chapter One we argued that an understanding of how arguments function in a legislative debate is crucial to successful advocacy. Thus far we have been concerned with the structure of arguments, the relationship among the essential components of an argument, and the tests to be applied to arguments. We are now prepared to discuss what to do when arguments for and against a proposed course of action are enjoined in a legislative setting.

The goal of any deliberative body is to have the best ideas emerge and survive. In fact, the survival of democratic institutions depends upon our willingness to challenge controversial proposals in the give-and-take of debate. If we believe that the United States should take actions against Japan to bring about fair trade, we ought to present our case for sanctions and defend our ideas as well as we can. If we believe that sanctions against Japan will be unwise, we ought to attack the proposal with all of the skills at our command. To shirk from our duty to engage in a meaningful clash of ideas is to be irresponsible.

It is not enough to construct initial arguments for or against a proposal, no matter how well they may be structured, supported, and presented. If we use arguments to test the probable truth of a position, these arguments must withstand the strongest possible attacks. In this chapter we will discuss what to do when you wish to challenge the arguments

of your opponents, and what to do when your arguments and those of your supporters are attacked. In the remainder of this chapter we will discuss (1) practical matters such as listening critically to the exchange of ideas during a debate, and keeping track of those ideas in a way that will allow you to comprehend the development of arguments throughout the debate; (2) the procedure used to attack or to defend an argument; (3) methods of attack and defense; and (4) the strategy of attack and defense.

Recognizing and Recording Arguments

Listening critically to the flow of arguments will enhance your ability to successfully attack and defend arguments. While it is beyond the scope of this book to provide a detailed and comprehensive treatment of listening, students who are interested in the subject will find a very practical resource in Richard A. Hunsaker's *Oral Communication: Speaking and Listening.*[1] Critical listening means listening for content and analyzing and evaluating the content as it is presented. Especially for beginning participants in Student Congress competition, this requires overcoming

the anxiety associated with competition. Too often students are so preoc-
cupied with the prepared statements they want to make that they miss
a great deal of what transpires in the debate. This accounts for speeches
that are largely repetitive of those that have been presented earlier and
that contribute little or nothing to the resolution of the controversy.
Even experienced debaters allow their emotions to interfere with their
ability to listen critically. They have preconceived attitudes about the
topic and when they hear arguments that they disagree with they become
so emotionally involved that they miss significant parts of the debate.
This leads to shallow or misdirected responses that do very little to move
the debate forward.

It is important that Student Congress participants learn to listen carefully from the outset of the debate until a final decision is made by the
legislative body. They cannot allow their attention to stray if they take
seriously the task of arriving at a critical decision. As they listen to
speeches, both pro and con, students should ask themselves: What was
actually said? What evidence did the speaker provide? Does the argument
support the position? Only then can we assess the strengths and weaknesses of the proposed course of action called for in a bill or resolution.
Critical listening is the first step toward responsible attack and defense.

Most Student Congress debates last an hour or more and many students participate in the give-and-take of arguments. To keep track of all
of the arguments presented, students must develop the ability to record
the "flow" of arguments. Craig R. Smith and David M. Hunsaker tell
us that "controversy is linear—that is, it moves forward. An idea is advanced; it is attacked. To defend that idea the attack must be answered.
The idea, newly refined, is then subject to attack again as, ideally, we
move closer and closer to the proper conclusion of the controversy."[2]

Because controversy is linear we can chart the development of individual arguments from the time they are introduced until the final response
is made. Students who fail to follow the development of an argument
will not be able to provide meaningful responses.

The test of any meaningful attack or defense of an argument is: Does
the response shift the argument back to the opposition? Mere repetition
of an argument will not suffice. An accurate recording of attack and
defense is necessary for success. We recommend the following plan for
recording the development of arguments in legislative debate.

1. Select an oversized sheet of paper and allow as much horizontal
   writing space as possible. On this sheet of paper provide columns for

recording arguments of individual speakers. Lengthy debates may require more than one page to record the development of arguments. A sample flow sheet follows:

Authorship	First Con	Pro	Con	Pro	Con
NAME	NAME	NAME	NAME	NAME	NAME

I.

   A.

      1.

      2.

   B.

      1.

      2.

      3.

II.

2. Outline arguments of the first speaker in the left column. This requires an ability to synthesize arguments so that they can be made compact and understandable. The notes on a flow chart will be simpler than the original argument but should get at the essence of what the speaker is saying. Returning to our sample NFL congress debate, we could record one major argument of Senator #1's opening speech as follows:

    I. Japan engages in unfair trade practices
      A. U.S. autos locked out of Japan (NYT)
        1. Japanese workers low pay
        2. Luxury tax penalizes U.S.
        3. Deficit in autos will worsen

If the source of the information is important, then the source should be recorded at the appropriate point in the outline of arguments. If the date of evidence is important, that should also be recorded.

3. In subsequent speeches, record the arguments not in the order in which they are presented, but parallel to the arguments that they attack or defend. If an entirely new argument is introduced, place it on the flow chart below existing arguments so that the linear development of this argument can be followed in subsequent speeches.

The flow chart should reveal at any time the current status of individual arguments. A good flow chart will not only allow you to determine who had the last say, but will also enable you to assess how well the argument has been developed. This is important because it lets you know what has yet to be answered if your position is to prevail. Finally, a good flow chart allows the debater to have a perspective on all of the arguments. You can see how lines of argument began, how arguments interrelate, and how they support the ultimate claim of a bill or resolution. Like any other skill, the skill of "flowing" arguments takes a great deal of practice. In time you will develop some shorthand techniques that will make flowing arguments easier (symbols such as # for number, = for equal, ↑ for increase and ↓ for decrease, and so forth. Topic-specific abbreviations can be used as well. For example, BOP for balance of payments and LT for luxury tax would be easy to remember. Abbreviations for newspapers and periodicals are common when flowing (NYT for *The New York Times* and NW for *Newsweek*). What is most important is that you be consistent in the use of these shorthand techniques so that you know what your symbols and abbreviations mean.

A line of argument could be flowed as follows:

BOP deficit the—U.S. consumers— —Japan laws———U.S. not——
result of unfair   prefer Japan   discrim against   adapt cars
trade. NYT '91   quality.   U.S. cars.   for Japan.

Keeping track of lines of argument as they develop throughout the debate on a bill or resolution is necessary if meaningful clash on the important issues is to take place. Without clash there can be no real testing of ideas, and a thoughtful decision by the legislative body will be very difficult if not impossible.

Procedures of Attack and Defense

The goal of attack and defense is to refute or reestablish issues critical to the outcome of the debate. Every debate will contain numerous arguments; some will be important, others will not be important. It is the task of each participant to determine which arguments need to be attacked and which arguments need to be defended. Attack and defense should not be an exercise confined to raising questions or sparring with your opponents. Refutation should be aimed at arguments that will weaken the position of your opponents. One way to overcome the urge to respond to every argument presented is to keep a careful flow chart of arguments so that you can determine which actually support the ultimate claim in the debate.

Once a decision to attack or defend an argument has been made, it is important that the attack or defense be clear to the members of the chamber. Far too often debaters engage in attack and defense in a random and disorganized manner that makes it difficult to follow the development of the refutation. A four-step procedure is recommended by many argumentation and debate texts to remedy this problem.

1. Tell your audience exactly what argument is being attacked or defended. Unless the audience knows what argument is being refuted, people will be confused and the impact of your refutation will be lost. This requires that the debater restate the argument clearly and concisely, preferably in the language of the opponent.

2. Present your attack or defense. State the claim you are advancing and provide any explanation needed to show how it refutes or rebuilds the argument.

3. Support your attack or defense. This can be done by presenting flaws in your opponent's arguments, by initiating new reasoning, or by presenting new evidence. Mere restatement of your original position without extending the argument will not suffice in most instances.

4. Explain *how* your attack or defense affects the ultimate claim in the debate. This fourth step is the most important and yet most overlooked in the procedure of attack and defense. This takes time to execute if properly done. In the long run, however, a few well-developed refutations that are clearly communicated will be more important than a barrage of objections that fail to address the central issues in a debate.

The following example shows how this four-step procedure could have been used in our sample NFL congress debate. Proponents of the resolution argue that Japan engages in unfair trade practices against the United States that have resulted in serious economic harms for America. To refute this claim, an opponent of the resolution could argue that Japan does not engage in unfair trade practices, and therefore our economic problems are the result of something other than Japanese trade policy. The attack would be presented as follows: "My opponent claims that Japan engages in unfair trade practices. I deny that this is the case. The facts are that the United States has trade policies toward Japan that are at least as unfair as those Japan employs. According to the March 2, 1992, issue of *U.S. News and World Report,* Japan's tariff for industrial products is 2.6%. America's, in case anyone is curious, is 3%, and according to the World Bank, Japan's nontariff barriers such as quotas and licenses are comparable to America's. Since our economic problems are not the result of Japanese trade policy, any attempts to apply economic sanctions against Japan will make matters worse, not better. A vote for the resolution will not solve our economic problems because the resolution is based on a faulty causal argument.''

Defense of an argument employs the same four-step process. If we use the above argument, a defense of unfair trade practices by Japan could be presented as follows: ''My opponent's argument does not deny that Japan engages in unfair trade practices. Selecting such measures of trade policy as tariffs on industrial goods and quotas and licenses and arguing that this proves that Japan does not engage in unfair trade is insufficient. The argument ignores specific trade policies that are unfair. Those of us who are supporting the resolution point to large government subsidies provided to Japanese corporations, to dock layovers of agricultural products, and to regulations that make American-made cars ill-suited for Japan. It is important to remember that there are many causes of our balance-of-trade deficit with Japan. The facts are that we have a large trade deficit with Japan and this deficit is caused by unfair trade practices. Unless we adopt the resolution, Japan will continue to use a variety of unfair trade practices.''

On more than one occasion we have stressed that arguments need to be extended during the process of attack and defense. Restating arguments that have already been made in a debate is largely a waste of everyone's time. Arguments are most often extended by providing counterevidence, counterarguments, or by taking an argument of your opponent and showing that it actually supports your position. Keeping track of arguments as they develop during the debate, making decisions to attack or defend only those arguments that are important to the outcome of the debate, and organizing your refutation by using the four-step procedure described above will help you compete effectively.

Methods of Attack and Defense

In Chapter One we explained that an argument consists of three components—claim, evidence, and inference. A primary way of attacking or defending an argument is to examine each of these component parts and the interrelationship among the parts to determine the soundness of the argument.

Claims, as you recall, are assertions that an advocate wants the audience to accept. Remember also that all policy claims are probability statements; that is, the claim always goes beyond the evidence. Because claims are not identical with the evidence provided to support them, you should ask yourself if the claim is warranted. Claims may not follow from the evidence presented, the relationship between the evidence and the claim may be unreasonable, and the claim may be weak or exaggerated. One way to expose a deficiency is to examine closely your opponent's use of evidence.

Claims are no stronger than the evidence on which they rest. If the evidence can be impugned, then the claim itself can also be questioned. The tests of evidence discussed in Chapter One need to be applied. Testimonial evidence, the type of evidence most often used in Student Congress competition, consists of statements by someone who is reporting what he has observed or statements that include his judgment about what he has observed. Both the competence and the credibility of the source need to be scrutinized. Competence has to do with a source's expertise on the matter about which he or she is testifying. An economist who offers an opinion about the impact of a particular protectionist trade measure may be wrong. If the economist does not have all the current and relevant data necessary to come to this conclusion, he could be defending his own philosophical position on protectionist policies that may apply generally but not to the specific situation. When we attack the opinion of any source we should ask, Who is the source? What are the source's specific qualifications? Is the opinion in the mainstream of other experts in the field?

Credibility has to do with source bias. When a source is employed to give an opinion, we should be skeptical. An economist in the employment of the political party in power may provide an interpretation that makes the economy look better than it actually is, and an economist employed by the opposition party may provide an interpretation that makes the economy appear worse. When an economist who is serving on the President's Council of Economic Advisers argues that the administration's economic policy is the best one for the nation to pursue, we need to balance that view with other available economic data. We should always ask, Does the source of the information have a vested interest in the outcome of the statement? Remember that newspapers and periodicals frequently have particular biases that need to be taken into account as well. Opinions offered by very conservative publications will differ from those opinions offered by very liberal publications.

There are several other tests of evidence that debaters should consider. We should ask if the evidence presented by each side in a controversy is internally consistent. If one argues during the course of a debate that foreign competition in the car market has improved the quality of American cars and has kept prices low, it would be inconsistent for one to advocate harsh import quotas that would severely restrict competition. Another consideration is whether the evidence is relevant or not. If one concludes that the Japanese engage in unfair trade practices with the United States and offers only a public-opinion poll to support the claim, an opponent could argue that public-opinion polls only measure what the public perceives to be true and that the general public does not have the relevant information necessary to make an accurate assessment of trade relations. How the public feels in this case is irrelevant. Finally, you should be attentive to evidence that is contradicted by other evidence. The size of the balance-of-payments deficit between the United States and Japan cannot be growing and shrinking at the same time. The deficit is either getting worse or it is getting better. If you follow the NFL Student Congress debate in Chapter One, you will notice that there is considerable confusion about the size of the balance-of-payments deficit between the United States and Japan. Verification is called for when evidence appears to be contradictory.

Another way of exposing deficient arguments is to apply the tests of inferences discussed in Chapter One. Remember that inferences provide the connection between evidence and claims and that the thought process involved must be reasonable. If a claim is based on too few or atypical examples, then we should, at a minimum, demand more proof. A stronger response would be to provide examples that weaken or disprove the claim. If there is evidence that Japan is importing American lumber and other raw materials in large quantities, the claim that Japan has closed its markets to the United States is partially offset.

If an analogy is weak—essential characteristics of the two items being compared are not comparable—the claim of the argument will be weak. If one argues that trade sanctions applied by the United States against Cuba prove that trade sanctions against Japan will also work, it would be easy to point up essential differences between Cuba and Japan to weaken the analogy.

When inferences from sign are used, you should ask if there are alternative explanations that better explain the relationship between the sign and the thing signified. A large balance-of-trade deficit may not be a sign of unfair trade practices; it may, for example, be the result of poor management practices in the American automobile industry.

Causal inferences, as we explained earlier, are complex. In the example we used earlier in this chapter, a causal argument is applicable. If your opponent ignores several of the multiple causes of unfair trade policies, you can argue that the claim has not been adequately refuted. Inferences from authority are based upon tests applied to the source of the evidence employed. Our discussion of evidence from testimony should suffice.

Keep in mind that an attack or defense can be both direct and indirect. Claims can be denied directly or a counterargument can be offered; evidence can be challenged directly or counterevidence can be presented to disprove the claim; the reasonableness of the inference can be directly questioned or an alternative explanation of the link between the evidence and claim can be offered.

Strategy of Attack and Defense

A common mistake that beginning debaters make is to think that every argument an opponent makes has to be challenged. Even experienced debaters spend time on arguments that are better ignored or dismissed. When you spend time quibbling over minor details that have little or nothing to do with the outcome of a debate, you run the risk of appearing argumentative, and your credibility is diminished. Waiting until a debate on a bill or resolution is under way before making decisions about which arguments must be attacked and which arguments must be defended invites disaster. While it may not be possible to anticipate every argument that will be introduced in a debate, a stock issues analysis (explained in Chapter Four) should help you determine what are the actual issues. Arguments that fail to address the vital issues are usually unimportant. The final decision in a debate should be based on the vital issues that provide the foundation for the ultimate claim.

Patterson and Zarefsky indicate that for each constructive argument, the debater has three choices: "You may ignore the argument, saying nothing about it. You may admit it, conceding its essential truth. Or you may attack it, choosing to develop and present a refutation."[3] If there is no advantage to be gained from attacking an argument, leave it alone. In our sample debate there are arguments that should be ignored and others that should be admitted. When Senator #15 argues that American farmers are not lazy, we have one example of an argument that should not be attacked. The dispute concerning workers in the debate centers on wage differentials and productiveness of people in the manufacturing sector, especially the automotive industry, of both the United States and Japan. Likewise, nothing can be gained by trying to deny what is obvious. That there is conflict over trade policies between the United States and Japan is apparent. What is not apparent is that support for the resolution will or will not diminish the conflict.

One should not spend time responding to arguments that are incidental to the outcome of the debate. Even if Senator #12's argument that the trade issue is being politicized by President Bush is true, this argument does not mean that trade imbalances do not exist and that no action is necessary to remedy the problem. The outcome of the debate will depend upon more substantive arguments, such as the size of the trade deficit, the causes of the trade deficit, and whether the proposed action will make matters worse or better.

Debaters should also keep in mind that it is not necessary to respond to each example of unfair trade practice if all of the examples can be refuted by attacking the generalization derived from the examples. If one can argue, as Senator #7 does, that it is a myth that our trade problems are made in Japan, then it is not necessary to attack individual examples of unfair trade practice. If our trade problems are the result of our own inability to manage our own economy, then the examples are of little consequence. Conversely, one need not attack a generalization based upon examples if one or more of the examples can be shown to be faulty.

Most of our discussion up to this point has focused on attacking rather than defending arguments. When defending an argument, you have more limited choices. Most often you have to respond to the attacks by your opponent no matter what kind of attack has been launched. The only exception is when the attack does not impair the argument or undermine the overall position that you advocate.

A different but frequently effective strategy of attack is to provide a counterargument. A counterargument does not challenge any component of your opponent's argument (claim, evidence, or inference) but develops an opposing position that denies the original claim. Senator #14 counters the argument that we need to buy more American cars to help solve our trade imbalance by arguing that we do not know what constitutes an American car: "The Ford Probe is built in Michigan by Mazda. The Plymouth Laser is built in Illinois by Mitsubishi. The Geo Prism is built in California by Toyota. The Mercury Tracer is imported from Mexico. . . . In the past decade Japanese automakers have transferred the production of 40% of their U.S. sales to America. This cost more than six billion dollars and created 39,000 new jobs." If counterarguments are lodged against your position, you will need to rebuild your position by refuting the counterargument or by explaining why the counterargument does not apply.

Summary

Because Student Congress speeches are very short, usually three minutes, the decisions you make about which arguments to attack or defend and about where to make the attack or defense, is crucial to success. Decisions of this magnitude should not be left to chance.

Preparation is very important. Planning begins with thorough research; you must identify the major issues in the topic and you must have a grasp of the evidence on both sides of the controversy. During the debate it is important that you listen critically and flow the debate. You will be presented with many choices. You will be successful only if you choose the right arguments to attack or defend.

Notes

1. Richard A. Hunsaker, *Oral Communication: Speaking and Listening* (Englewood, Colo.: Morton, 1990).

2. Craig R. Smith and David M. Hunsaker, *The Bases of Argument* (Indianapolis: Bobbs-Merrill, 1972), 204.

3. J. W. Patterson and David Zarefsky, *Contemporary Debate* (Boston: Houghton Mifflin, 1983), 76.

Discussion Questions

1. Explain the difference between extending an argument and repeating an argument.

2. Discuss the limitation of a point-by-point refutation of an opponent's speech.

3. What are the advantages of having a negative constructive position if you are opposed to the bill or resolution being debated?

4. What are the advantages and disadvantages of using the recommended four-step method for refuting arguments?

5. Which element—attack or defense—is more important in a legislative debate?

6. How can you detect inconsistent arguments presented by your opponents during a debate?

7. Discuss the relative merits of attacking the evidence, the claim, or the inference of an argument.

8. Explain the statement, Critical listening is essential to effective attack and defense.

9. Discuss the statement, Attack and defense should work to establish the probability of what is true and to reveal the inadequacies of what is false.

10. What is the implication of the statement that "controversy is linear" for flowing arguments in a legislative debate?

CHAPTER 3

Researching Student Congress Legislation

The ability of a legislative body to arrive at critical decisions is directly related to the quality of information that is provided by the participants. Debate, properly practiced, is a fact-centered process. Because evidence is the foundation on which a claim rests, one should begin the study of a subject by seeking out facts rather than relying on guesses or assumptions. Conclusions that fail to square with the facts should be rejected.

Reaching a critical decision when complex policy claims are the subject of debate requires a large supply of many different sorts of facts— statistics, examples, historical data, existing laws or treaties, and expert opinion or predictions. While the ability to develop and present persuasive arguments in a debate is important, research is the most essential part of the activity. First, any attempt to influence other people without making sure that your knowledge is adequate and your analysis thoughtful is irresponsible. Second, careful research is necessary for practical reasons. A debater is not likely to prevail in the give-and-take of debate without substantial support for arguments. Finally, participants in a legislative debate are quick to sense when a debater is not prepared. To be ill-informed is to run the risk of losing one's credibility.

A Student Congress participant becomes a debater long before standing to speak for or against a proposed action. Most of the research,

analysis, and evaluation of the subject will remain hidden from view. Only a fraction of the information uncovered will be used in a debate. However, without the labor that goes into acquiring knowledge, debaters will not have their ideas prevail. Locating, collecting, recording, and organizing relevant data are the subjects of this chapter.

Sources of Information

Participants in Student Congress rely most heavily on written sources for the evidence they use in debates. Written sources include books, documents, reference works, periodicals, newspapers, and material such as pamphlets. Of these, periodicals, newspapers, and some specific reference works are generally the best choices. Books contain information that is often out of date, and it takes considerable time to read through a book to obtain information. Original documents, while they are a rich source of information on a wide variety of topics, are difficult to obtain unless you have access to a major library or a library that has been designated a government-documents depository. Unless you have a great deal of time to research a topic, congressional hearings and reports are not practical resources. Encyclopedias may be of some value if you need a brief historical perspective on a topic; however, the material will often be out of date.

Periodicals are a valuable resource for current topics. Magazines are periodicals that are written to appeal to a wide reading audience. Most of the articles are short and are written in nontechnical language that the general public can read and understand. The general news weeklies, such as *Time, Newsweek,* and *U.S. News and World Report*, are valuable for keeping abreast of current developments. Reading one or more of these magazines each week is an excellent way of developing a broad understanding of current events.

Journals are intended for a more limited reading audience. Frequently, the language is more technical and the style more complex. The articles are most often written by scholars and represent in-depth research. Journals provide analysis and insight that can be very useful to Student Congress participants. Examples of scholarly journals include *Journal of the American Medical Association, Political Science Quarterly,* and *American Bar Association Journal.* Articles in journals contain bibliographies that can lead a debater to other valuable material.

Periodical literature is valuable because it constitutes the majority of published information available. There are thousands of periodicals published regularly and they contain some of the most recent information that can be found. Periodical literature reflects contemporary opinion as well as the constantly evolving nature of controversial subjects.

There are many indexes that can be consulted to find periodical literature. *The Reader's Guide to Periodical Literature* is an index that includes many subjects and, for the most part, indexes popular magazines. The main body of the index consists of subject and author entries listed alphabetically. Other periodical indexes, such as *Applied Science and Technology Index, Business Index, Psychological Abstracts, Social Sciences Index, Education Index,* and *Humanities Index* deal principally with one subject area and index journals with scholarly articles. Most of the paper versions of periodical indexes are published monthly with annual accumulations.

Newspapers are so varied that it is difficult to generalize concerning which of them will be most useful. *The New York Times* continues to set the standard because its coverage is more comprehensive than that of most newspapers and because it publishes its own index. *The New*

York Times contains reports on congressional committee hearings, reports on Supreme Court decisions when the court is in session, and the Sunday edition contains a useful section called "The Week in Review." Because major news items appear in newspapers on the same day or the following day, *The New York Times Index* can be used to find materials in other newspapers that are not indexed. The *Christian Science Monitor, Wall Street Journal, Washington Post, Los Angeles Times,* and *Chicago Tribune* are good newspapers that contain interpretations and evaluations of current news.

Reference books vary widely. Thousands of reference materials are published each year in the form of dictionaries, encyclopedias, almanacs and yearbooks, handbooks and manuals, guidebooks, directories, and bibliographies. Student Congress participants should get to know the reference librarian. These specialists are trained to analyze the research needs of students and can assist you in locating different kinds of materials. Before approaching a reference librarian, students should have a clear idea of what kinds of materials they need. Valuable time is lost if you have only a vague notion of what you need. Most libraries have one or more guides to reference books, which list reference sources by subject, that can be consulted as well.

The quality of reference works varies widely and students need to exercise some critical judgment regarding reference materials. You should determine if the article in the reference work is written by an authority in the field, if the material is current, if it is objective, and if the factual data is documented. There is an important difference between reference materials that are based upon primary sources and those that rely on secondary sources. Student Congress participants need to be aware of several important reference works that can prove beneficial. *Roget's Thesaurus of English Words and Phrases* will provide you with synonyms that can be useful when you go "online" to do keyword research. Keyword searching is discussed later in this chapter. An unabridged dictionary, such as *Webster's Third New International Dictionary of the English Language*, is a comprehensive and authoritative reference, and *Black's Law Dictionary*, an example of a subject dictionary, defines terms used in law and related fields. Almanacs and yearbooks, such as *Information Please Almanac, Atlas and Yearbook; The World Almanac and Book of Facts;* and *Statistical Abstract of the United States* are useful reference works that provide information on a wide range of subjects. Statistics in these reference works are most often from primary sources and the information is documented. These reference works are updated annually.

Electronic Technologies

Technology will continue to have a major impact on information storage and retrieval. To be an efficient researcher, one has to be alert to modifications in existing library electronic information sources as well as to newly created databases and new formats. Many libraries have automated catalogues, optical disk (CD-ROM) databases, and subscriptions to one or more online database services. Some libraries are part of an electronic network for the purpose of sharing resources.

Automated catalogues are the most common form of electronic storage and retrieval. These catalogues contain records of materials in the library in much the same way as a card catalogue. Online databases are another important form of information storage and retrieval. These databases are created by academic associations, government agencies, and commercial enterprises. They can provide bibliographic information, abstracts, and full text. Most of the online databases are available by subscription through vendors such as Dialog or H. W. Wilson. Hundreds of the most popular online databases are now available on CD-ROM (compact disc–read only memory). These disks are used to store a variety of information including indexes, census data, maps, and literary works. The great advantage of CD-ROM technology is that a vast amount of information (approximately 250,000 printed pages) can be stored and quickly accessed from a 4.75-inch disk. CD-ROM systems are not as expensive as online systems, yet they offer the same ease of use. Most libraries do not charge patrons to use CD-ROM databases. Simple searches can usually be performed without the assistance of a reference librarian once a patron is acquainted with the system. The principal disadvantage of a CD-ROM system is that it is not updated as frequently as an online database.

The *TOM* (text on microform) *CD-ROM Index* is a database designed specifically for secondary-level students. Although the *TOM Index* references many fewer periodicals than *Reader's Guide*, it includes coverage of political events, business, social science, and consumer issues. The index provides citations keyed to the full text of articles on microfiche. An onscreen help menu outlines search and print procedures. Subject headings (a subject, a person, place, or event) are used to search the *TOM Index*. Subheadings are used to narrow the search. A more complete discussion of the *TOM Index* can be found in the October 1990 issue of *School Library Journal*.[1] *InfoTrac* is a periodical index on a CD-ROM disk that is updated monthly. This computer-run index includes citations to over half a million articles from more than a thousand popular magazines and business and professional journals. *Reader's Guide to Periodical Literature* on CD-ROM (WILSONDISC) indexes general magazines that cover all subject areas. *ABI/Inform* on CD-ROM is an example of an index that includes only business and trade journals. The CD-ROM version includes abstracts with citations and allows keyword searching.

It is imperative that researchers become familiar with computers and the kinds of information available in electronic format. Electronic database sources are particularly important to Student Congress participants for four reasons:

- Electronic databases can be searched more quickly and more efficiently than paper indexes.

- These databases hold more information and they are updated frequently.

- Many databases store the full text of articles that may not be available in print form in a local library.

- The databases permit searching by keywords as well as by subject or author, something which is not possible using print sources.

CD-ROM and Online Searching

Not all systems have the same features or commands. Simple written commands to access the system, CD-ROM, or online databases are most often available at the computer terminal and these commands are supplemented by user guides or onscreen menus. Because online searching is expensive, a librarian familiar with the online system usually assists with the search. Most systems allow for *author search, title search, subject search,* and *keyword search.* Subject heading and keyword searching are especially useful for students participating in Student Congress. Keyword searching, in particular, allows you to find information when you have partial or incomplete information. For example, if only the last name of an author is known, if only part of a title is known, or if the correct subject heading is not known, a keyword search will allow you to locate information. A method for finding keywords to research bills and resolutions is detailed in Chapter Four.

CD-ROM and online databases are available on a wide variety of subjects that include a number of kinds of information. For students participating in legislative debate the most important kinds of information include

- indexes, which give citations for periodical articles, newspaper articles, books, government reports, and so forth;

- abstracts, which give citations plus a summary with sufficient information for the reader to determine whether the article is appropriate;

- full text of newspaper articles, periodical articles, some court cases, research reports, and so forth.

Many databases include a thesaurus listing vocabulary from the database to make a subject or keyword search more efficient.

Before approaching a librarian to get help for a database search, students should have prepared a search strategy. This will include a debate proposition derived from a study of the bill or resolution, subject terms, keywords, databases to be searched, and dates or time frames. A librarian who is familiar with database searching can help refine the search strategy to accomplish the research goals. When the search strategy is entered into the computer, information indicating the number of citations located will appear within seconds. Depending on what is available in the database, one can request source citations, source citations plus abstracts, or the full text of articles.

One way to ensure a successful search is to prepare a search worksheet. An example of a search worksheet can be found in *Classmate: Student Workbook*, prepared by Dialog Information Services, Inc.[2] The value of a search worksheet is that it reminds you to include all the data you need for a database search. A search strategy will include the following steps:

1. Determine the broad topic to be searched.

2. Select the databases to be used.

3. Determine the keywords to be used in the search.

4. Structure your database search using Boolean operators: **and, or,** and **not**.

Student Congress participants should study and analyze a bill or resolution to determine what the controversy is and what must be done to resolve the controversy. A stock issues analysis, discussed in Chapter

Four, will help you make this determination. A final product of this analysis should be a debatable proposition. An analysis of "A Resolution Concerning Japanese Trade" would result in a debate proposition such as, "Resolved: That the United States should apply trade sanctions against Japan to bring about fair trade."

Since the task is to locate materials that are current and readily available, we suggest using a periodical index and a newspaper index. The *TOM CD-ROM Index* references approximately 100 magazines, Dialog's *Magazine Index* indexes 435 general and popular periodicals, and Dialog's *Academic Index* includes 400 academic journals. Dialog's *Newsearch* indexes 1,800 newspapers, wire services, magazines, business publications, and computer and legal periodicals.

Studying the bill or resolution and reading an article or two on the general topic should help you identify subject headings and several keywords. Once the database search has started, you can find additional and sometimes more useful keywords by referring to "descriptors" that are included with the citations and abstracts of articles. Keywords that would be obvious after initial study of the above debate proposition would include *United States, Japan, trade, tariffs, quotas, subsidies, sanctions,* and *deficits.* Since our goal is to get current data, it is important to enter a time frame for the search as well, for example, 1991–1992.

The final step is to refine the search using Boolean operators. The **and** operator tells the computer to search for articles by combining ideas represented by keywords, such as United **and** States **and** Japan **and** trade **and** py = 1991:1992. (The *py* stands for publication year.) The operator **and** narrows the search. Articles published during the last two years are desirable. Each database service has its own way to limit searches.

The **or** operator tells the computer to search terms that can be used interchangeably, such as tariff **or** duty. The information you want can be found under either keyword. The **or** operator broadens the search. The **not** operator tells the computer to exclude a term from the search, such as trade **not** rice. The **not** operator further limits a search. A more complete discussion of Boolean operators can be found in Dialog's *Classmate: Student Workbook.*[3]

The example below illustrates how Boolean operators are used in an online search in Dialog's *Magazine Index.* The researcher is seeking recent information in the database that pertains to trade between the United States and Japan. Computer commands vary from one service to another. We used **begin, find, type,** and **logoff.** Once into the database the researcher connects United **and** States **and** Japan **and** Trade **and** py = 1991:1992. The computer responds by displaying the number of times each keyword appears in the database, followed by the set that shows the number of citations featuring all of the keywords.

	219883	UNITED	/number of documents found/
	192901	STATES	
	15125	JAPAN	
	37250	TRADE	
	275559	PY = 1991:1992	
set 1	169	UNITED AND STATES AND JAPAN AND TRADE AND 1991:2	

To further narrow the search the computer was instructed to find only those sources in set 1 that provide an **analysis** (set 2) of the subject. Find set 1 and 2.

set 3   23   set 1 and set 2

Twenty-three of the 169 articles in set 1 contained an analysis of the subject.

The researcher then commanded the computer to find tariff **or** duty:

	850	TARIFF
	1188	DUTY
set 4	2006	TARIFF OR DUTY

This command broadened the search to find all articles that contain both keywords: tariff or duty (set 4).

The next request was to find set 1 and set 4:

set 5   2   set 1 and set 4

When set 1 and set 4 were combined, two citations were found in the database (set 5).

Finally, a request was made to find set 1 **not** rice:

	169	set 1
	2026	RICE
set 6	164	set 1 NOT RICE

Five citations were deleted from the 169 citations in set 1 when "not rice" was included in the command to produce set 6.

Student Congress Online Database Search Worksheet

Title of bill or resolution: _____

ILL: Problem—nature, scope, harms. _____

_____

BLAME: Cause(s). _____

_____

CURE: Solution. _____

_____

COST: Consequences of solution. _____

_____

Debatable proposition: _____

_____

Keywords: _____   _____   _____

_____   _____   _____

Databases: _____   _____   _____

Boolean Operators: (AND—OR—NOT)

_____ AND _____ AND _____ AND _____

_____ OR _____

_____ NOT _____

COMMAND STATEMENTS: Follow computer terminal instructions.

Blank worksheet form.

Student Congress Online Database Search Worksheet

Title of bill or resolution: *"A Resolution Concerning Japanese Trade"*

ILL: Problem—nature, scope, harms.   *Trade deficit, Economic impacts, Unemployment, Industrial decline.*

BLAME: Cause(s).   *Tariffs, Quotas, Government subsidies, Dock layovers, Licensing procedures.*

CURE: Solution.   *Apply Trade sanctions against Japan.*

COST: Consequences of solution.   *Protectionist trade policies, Trade War, Reduced balance-of-trade deficit, Fair trade.*

Debatable proposition: *"Resolved: That the United States should apply trade sanctions against Japan to bring about fair trade."*

Keywords: *United States, Japan, Trade, Deficit, Tariffs, Quotas, Sanctions, Protectionism, Subsidies, Dock layovers, Automobiles.*

Databases: *Magazine Index, Academic Index, Newspaper Index*

Boolean Operators: (AND—OR—NOT)

United States AND	*Japan*	AND	*Trade*	AND *py 1991:1992*
	Tariffs	OR	*Duties*	
	Trade	NOT	*Rice*	

COMMAND STATEMENTS: Follow computer terminal instructions.

Completed worksheet form.

After you have narrowed your search and made a determination of the information you want, print the citations of the sources, print citations with abstracts, or print full text of articles if they are available and cost-effective. You may want to start with citations that include abstracts if you need additional keywords to further refine the search. Below is an example of a citation with an abstract taken from the *National Newspaper Index* (some extraneous data is deleted in the following citation).

DIALOG File 111: NATIONAL NEWSPAPER INDEX
Marketing in Japan made simple. (goal is to produce desirable products) (Editorial)
Los Angeles Times v111 col 3 pB4 Jan 13, 1992
DESCRIPTORS: United States—Relations with Japan; Japan—Relations with the United States; Free trade and protection—Analysis; Product development—International aspects

Although online searching can be expensive and searching by keywords can sometimes retrieve articles that are not relevant to the specific needs of the researcher, the advantages are very significant. Online searching is flexible and saves time. The databases are updated frequently and they are designed to permit keyword searching with Boolean operators to narrow the search in ways that printed sources do not allow. Online searching also provides access to a large number of databases containing materials that even large libraries do not house. Finally, a researcher can acquire a printout of the desired information without having to write out citations from paper indexes.

Our next task is to select the materials that are most suitable and arrange them in a format that will facilitate their use in a Student Congress competition.

Student Congress participants face several obstacles that need to be addressed. First, there are many bills and resolutions (frequently twenty-five to thirty separate bills and resolutions) that have to be researched. Second, the time available to research these bills and resolutions is limited (often, only a few weeks). No one person, with all the demands of being a full-time student, can research twenty-five to thirty topics in a period of a month and be prepared to debate each of these bills and resolutions with confidence. Individual members of a Student Congress group must share the responsibility for all members of the group being prepared to debate well. While it is often true that among twenty-five to thirty bills and resolutions there are a few topic duplications, and while a few bills and resolutions can be discounted because they are not really suitable for debate, the task is still formidable.

The Research Packet

Our suggestion is that the bills and resolutions be divided among the total congress squad and that each member research at least one bill or resolution, depending on the size of the group. If your group is very large you may want to assign two persons to research one bill or resolution. It is our opinion that a uniform format be employed by all research participants. We have discussed at length the process of locating materials for Student Congress. The next task is to locate the best sources available, and then to carefully read and analyze these sources, being careful to select materials representing both sides of the controversy.

Once this is accomplished the researchers need to prepare a research packet that can be effectively used by all members of the squad. The following items must be included in the packet:

1. A copy of the bill or resolution.

2. A synopsis of the bill or resolution. The synopsis should include the objectives of the bill or resolution, any historical background necessary to understand arguments in the context of the controversy, and comments regarding the nature of the controversy, including which side appears to be stronger if there is better evidence on one side of the controversy. If it appears that the bill or resolution can be strengthened by an amendment, the recommended amendment should be included.

3. A list of pro arguments and con arguments. Every argument that can be advanced on either side of the controversy should be included. Seek to arrange the arguments so that for each pro argument there is a parallel con argument. These should be presented as succinct argument statements.

4. Evidence from research with source citations to support each argument. At the top of the page, number the argument and include the argument statement. Use a separate sheet of paper for each argument. Start with the first pro argument and follow this with succeeding pro arguments. Con arguments follow in order. A cut-and-paste system can be used to save time. Cut evidence statements from photocopies of articles and place on the page following the argument statement. Remember that you need to type in the source citation for each piece of evidence.

5. A select bibliography or photocopies of articles. Complete source citations for several pro articles and several con articles or photocopies of
   these articles should be the final item in the packet. (If photocopies of
   articles are included, it is imperative that you abide by copyright laws.
   School and "fair use" copyright law applies. See *The Official Fair-Use
   Guidelines*, Copyright Information Services, Harbor View Publications Group, Friday Harbor, Wash.) Having a copy of the articles
   available makes it possible for students who have not done the research
   to understand the arguments contained in the research packet.

A SAMPLE RESEARCH PACKET FOR STUDENT CONGRESS

Following is a sample of each of the items to be included in the recommended research packet. However, space does not permit us to include
multiple pages of evidence and photocopies of articles. The following
items are taken from an actual student research assignment:

A Bill to Use Tax Laws to Limit Population Growth

1	Article 1	Each family shall be limited to two natural
2		children.
3	Article 2	"Natural" shall be defined as a biological child of
4		one of the parents.
5	Article 3	Federal tax laws will be changed to penalize
6		families that have more than two children. If a
7		family has a third child, they will be able to
8		claim only one child dependent; if a fourth, none.
9		Families who have more than four children will be
10		assessed a $500 tax liability for each
11		additional child.
12	Article 4	This bill shall take effect in 1994.
13	Article 5	The enforcement of this bill will be the
14		responsibility of the Internal Revenue Service.
15	Article 6	All laws in conflict with this bill are hereby
16		declared null and void.

Submitted to the
Committee on Economics

Author's name
Author's school

Synopsis

This bill seeks to limit population growth in the United States by using federal tax laws to penalize parents who have more than two biological children. Currently a family may claim all of its children as dependents on the federal tax form, which results in a lower tax assessment. In states where the total tax liability for the state is tied to the federal tax liability, the penalty would increase. The bill is vague about what would happen if two single parents, each with two or more biological children, married. One might argue that the penalties prescribed in the bill would apply.

The topic is controversial. There are a number of arguments that can be advanced to limit population growth. The environment is negatively affected as population grows, especially in a developed nation where each person consumes and disposes of large quantities of materials. As job creation diminishes, the need to reduce the size of the work force is an important consideration. As income declines for many families there is a need to limit family size in order to provide for the necessities of life. You can also argue that the cost of government increases as the size of the population increases, and given our large federal deficit, we can no longer afford to allow population to grow. Finally, you can argue that the United States needs to set a good example for the rest of the world, especially for Third World countries, where population growth is excessive.

Those who oppose the bill can argue that the population in the United States is growing more slowly than at any time in our history. You can also argue that there are better means of improving the environment than limiting population growth. Rather than limiting population, we should work to increase job and income growth to solve our economic problems. Federal programs that discourage productivity are a better target than population growth. The United States can be more successful in helping Third World nations reduce their population growth by providing those countries with technologies to limit births and improve the environment. Finally, this bill may result in more abortions and may have an impact on adoptions.

PRO ARGUMENTS	CON ARGUMENTS
1. Limiting population growth will improve the environment.	1. Bill will have little or no impact on the environment.
2. There are not enough jobs to sustain population growth.	2. Job creation is independent of stable population growth.

3. Falling incomes argue for smaller families.

3. Creating good jobs will improve incomes.

4. Federal expenses grow as population grows.

4. Improved federal programs will cost less and a larger work force will increase revenues.

5. The U.S. should set a good example for Third World countries.

5. Direct population control efforts will be successful.

6. Bill will result in more adoptions.

6. Bill will result in more abortions.

PRO ARGUMENT #1:   Limiting population growth will improve the environment.

"By any measure, the U.S. already is vastly overpopulated. We long since have exceeded the long-range carrying capacity of our resources and environment, yet we continue to grow rapidly, by about 25,000,000 each decade."

Donald Mann, President, Negative Population Growth, Inc., in "Why We Need a Smaller U.S. Population." *USA Today*, Sept. 1992, p. 37.

Several pieces of evidence should be included for each argument statement. Choose evidence that specifically supports the argument, and choose evidence from several sources. Remember that your colleagues depend on your selection of evidence to argue the bill or resolution.

There is no magical formula for determining how many pieces of evidence should be included for each argument statement. There will be lots of evidence to support some arguments and less evidence to support other arguments, depending on the topic being debated. The more quality evidence you can supply, the better.

Include one or more pages of evidence with citations for each pro and each con argument.

Bibliography or Photocopies of Articles

1.   Mann, Donald, "Why We Need a Smaller U.S. Population."
USA Today, September 1992, 37.

A select bibliography should be included that will allow participants to find
and read a few articles that provide good evidence, both pro and con, on the
bill or resolution. If photocopies of articles can be included in the packet, this
saves time. Make sure copyright laws are followed if articles are included.

Summary

Student Congress participants cannot succeed without engaging in serious research. In this chapter we emphasize the need to locate written
sources that provide the most current data available on controversial
topics. Periodicals, newspapers, and select reference works are the most
promising sources. Printed indexes can be used to locate periodical,
newspaper, and reference-work articles, but they do not offer the same
advantages as electronic database searches. Subject heading and keyword searching in databases make it possible to find materials quickly
and efficiently. The use of Boolean operators allows the researcher to
refine the search in ways not possible when using printed indexes. Preparing a database worksheet is a prerequisite to a successful search.

We recommend that a standard format for recording debate research
be used to facilitate its use by members of a Student Congress group. The
task of researching a large number of topics in a short period of time requires a strategy for dealing with a large quantity of information. Obviously, the quality of a research packet is dependent on the individual researcher. The more often you engage in research and in putting together
a research packet, the more proficient you will become. Remember that
the success of the group is linked to the quality of individual work.

Notes

1. "Computer Software Review," *School Library Journal* (October
    1990), 62.

2. *Classmate: Student Workbook* (Palo Alto, Calif.: Dialog Information Services, February 1987), 22.

3. Ibid., 24–26.

Discussion Questions

1. Discuss the role of the reference librarian as an important resource in a library.

2. Why is it important to read the preliminary pages in a book before proceeding to the text?

3. Discuss the advantages and disadvantages of a card catalogue, an online catalogue, and a CD-ROM catalogue.

4. Discuss the differences between keyword indexing and subject indexing.

5. Why is it important for a researcher to determine the date of the reference source being used?

6. Why are newspapers and periodicals important sources for Student Congress research?

7. What are the advantages of using an abstract index rather than a citation index when doing research?

8. Discuss the steps involved in conducting an online search, including the use of Boolean operators.

9. Discuss the advantages of online searching in comparison with manual searching. Are there any disadvantages to online searching?

10. Discuss the purpose of documentation in an argumentative speech.

CHAPTER 4

Preparing Student Congress Legislation

Before a bill or resolution reaches the floor of the United States Congress for debate, a great deal of preliminary committee work is completed. These committees identify the nature and extent of the problem, examine current laws that apply to the problem, and make a determination as to what action is needed to solve the problem. Only after extensive hearings are completed and reports prepared is the bill or resolution drafted. The bill or resolution becomes the focus of the debate.

Ideally, Student Congress follows many of the same procedures. Although formal hearings are not completed and reports are not prepared by Student Congress participants, it is necessary that thoughtful study and analysis go into student-written legislation.

This chapter will concentrate on preparing legislation suitable for competition. Four specific areas will be discussed:

- locating controversial topics for legislative debate;

- conducting preliminary topic research to determine debatability;

- deciding if the topic can best be presented as a bill or a resolution;

- writing legislation for Student Congress competition.

Locating Controversial Topics for Legislative Debate

A prerequisite to becoming a successful Student Congress participant is to develop and maintain an interest in current events. This can be accomplished by reading at least one major newspaper a day, consistently attending to broadcast news, and scanning one or two news periodicals a week. Because Student Congress legislation focuses on a variety of topics it is important to have a broad perspective on current events. For example, legislation calling for a significant increase in our welfare expenditures, although desirable, may preclude spending on a deteriorating infrastructure or other problems. Without a comprehensive understanding of current events, a participant may not recognize that the solution to welfare could negatively affect other social and economic areas.

Once you have a grasp of current events, it will be helpful to meet with a group of other students who will be competing in Student Congress. This group may be composed of your classmates or teammates. The presence of an instructor or a sponsor will be helpful in keeping the group on task. The purpose of this group meeting is to brainstorm a list of possible topics that may be suitable for legislation. Initially, no topic should be discounted. All group members should be encouraged to introduce ideas, no matter how foolish they seem. An attempt to compile and record an all-inclusive list of topics should be the group's first responsibility.

The list will serve as a starting point for determining which of these topics are significant and controversial. Controversial claims are present when a substantial difference of opinion exists. Because we can never be absolutely certain of future action, especially in the area of public policy, it is important to weigh controversy surrounding the nature of the problem, causes that contribute to the problem, new proposals for solving the problem, and benefits to be gained by the new proposals (see Chapter One, *Contemporary Debate*).[1] By analyzing these areas of potential conflict, you will avoid trivial topics. If, for example, you were considering the qualifications of presidential candidates for office, a focus on the qualifications of their spouses would become trivial. On the other hand, if one of the topics is homelessness, it is important for your group to determine which aspects of the problem will provide clash and will be worthy of debate. Given the data available, most individuals would agree that the problem is significant. The controversy would likely focus on a feasible solution to the problem of homelessness and who should assume responsibility for the solution.

Not only do new topics serve as an initial starting point for writing bills and resolutions, but Student Congress legislation that has been debated at previous competitions may be reconsidered to reflect new realities. For example, the issue of abortion has long been debated in this country and is yet to be resolved. State restrictions on abortion (e.g., Pennsylvania and Missouri) have recently been brought before the Supreme Court and most of these challenges to *Roe v. Wade* were upheld. The Court's interpretation allowed states to impose "reasonable restrictions" on *Roe v. Wade*.[2] Current legislation could center on the rights of the states to pass laws restricting abortions. These court challenges have had a dramatic impact on both the pro-life and pro-choice movements in the country and have provided a new perspective of current interest.

Another issue that has been debated over and over is across-the-board cuts in defense spending. Typically, Student Congress legislation will propose arbitrary reductions ranging anywhere from ten to fifteen percent. As a result, the debate becomes trivialized, with the Student Congress participants arguing that one prescribed cut is better than another. A way to improve this debate is to change the perspective. Legislation based on the end of the Cold War and the breakup of the former Soviet

Union should bring a shift in focus. For instance, a piece of legislation could advocate that the European community assume the major support of Allied troops stationed in Europe. One could argue that it is no longer fair to ask the United States to pay the substantial portion of the defense costs of NATO when the European nations are financially sound. They should provide for their own defense.

These are only two examples of frequently debated topics that could be rewritten with a new emphasis. Maintaining a file of previously debated legislation will provide ideas for topics. A rule of thumb would be to rewrite legislation only if new information and a new focus warrant debating the same topic area. The next step after selecting suitable topics for legislation is to conduct preliminary research to determine if the topic is, in fact, debatable.

Conducting Preliminary Topic Research to Determine Debatability

Well-balanced debate in Student Congress competition begins with controversial topics. A sound way of determining if the topic you have selected is truly debatable is to conduct preliminary research in your school or community library. This can easily be done by using newspaper and periodical indices. Chapter Three will assist you with this research. It is helpful to compile a list of key words (that is, cross-reference words) when searching your general topic area. These key words will assist you in locating controversial issues related to the general topic area. For example, if you were researching abortion, it would prove beneficial to examine entries under *Roe v. Wade*, *Webster v. Reproductive Services*, *Pennsylvania v. Casey*, RU-486, pro-life, pro-choice, and so forth. Scrutinizing the number of entries under the main and subordinate headings will help you to determine whether or not the topic is suitable for debate. If there are only a few listings, the topic probably will not allow for clash in a Student Congress debate. Preparing a topic for debate with limited information available to students will result in poor debate. Conversely, if there are many listings there is a good chance that this topic will provide for good debate.

Not only does a wealth of entries indicate that a particular issue is debatable, but the titles of the entries may also help you decide if the issues are of a controversial nature. The titles will often be an indication of the authors' position either for or against a given topic. If abstracts (short summaries of article content) are available, they will be a better indication of whether real controversy on the topic exists. A good topic will be recent, significant, and controversial. Read over the general headings once again in order to determine if there is a balance in the number of articles written on both sides of the topic. If there is, then the ability to locate information on both sides of the debate should be relatively easy.

Once you have reviewed the printed information that appears in the indices, you are ready to choose several articles that have been written on the subject. Select articles based on their titles and abstracts. Remember to choose articles on both sides of the topic. This preliminary reading will prepare you to use a method called stock issues analysis.

STOCK ISSUES ANALYSIS

A stock issues analysis raises questions to help you uncover the actual issues in a debate.

Ill. When analyzing a policy proposal, you ask the following questions: Is there a problem? Is the problem widespread? Is the problem significantly harmful?

Blame. Then you ask questions that try to get at the cause: What causes the problem? Is there a single cause, or are there multiple causes? Is the problem a result of existing policy or does the problem exist because we do not have legislation to bring about needed changes?

Cure. Questions that focus on a solution include: How can the problem best be solved? What actions are required? Who will be responsible for solving the problem? What will it take to solve the problem? Who will enforce the policy? What power will they be given?

Costs. Finally, you need to ask questions about the potential costs: Will the solution to the problem bring about significant advantages? Will any disadvantages result? Since legislative debate proposes some type of future action, asking questions represented by the stock issues will assist you in discovering actual issues vital to the problem area. Ultimately, reasonable people accept future risks only if there is a strong probability that the proposed changes will be beneficial.

Let us take an actual controversy, the recent restrictions placed on abortion by the Supreme Court. Student Congress legislation on this particular topic could be written either to outlaw abortions or to give women the right to choose without state intervention. Assuming we propose outlawing abortions, the stock issues would assist us in determining the actual issues in the controversy.

For example, we could argue that the problem is significant because 1.5 million abortions are performed each year in the United States. Additionally, we could argue that the recent Supreme Court interpretation regarding restrictions will not materially affect the total number of abortions. Abortions destroy lives and women who have abortions suffer psychological harm. Whole families are adversely affected.

We could also argue that the cause of the problem is not dealt with. The *Roe v. Wade* decision, which allows abortions during the first trimester, continues to be the law, and people who want abortions will not be dissuaded by recent Supreme Court rulings. These rulings are only a minor inconvenience. The major disadvantage is that people will be fooled into believing that we have dealt with the abortion issue, when, in fact, we have not. The only way to solve the problem is to outlaw abortions except in cases of rape, incest, or harm to the mother. The advantages to be gained from a ban are significant reductions in the number of abortions performed, and a reduction in harm suffered by women who have abortions and the harm suffered by their families.

Remember, you are not debating the stock issues. The stock issues are simply an analytical tool for discovering the actual issues inherent in the topic.

Deciding If the Topic Can Best Be Presented As a Bill or a Resolution

Student Congress legislation takes two forms: bills and resolutions. Just as the United States Congress debates bills and resolutions, Student Congress debates student-written bills and resolutions.

A bill creates new law. Basically, it addresses a current problem and suggests a course of action for solving the problem, or it provides a course of action to bring about benefits that will not result without the specific proposal. Bills include articles (sometimes the word *section* will be substituted for the word *article* in a bill).

A standard format for writing a Student Congress bill is presented below. This generic example will provide a description of each major component of a bill. Article I of a bill specifically states the new policy action (in an affirmative declarative sentence). Article II clarifies any ambiguous terms in Article I to avoid misunderstanding. The remaining articles offer the logistics for implementing the new policy. Article III sets the time when the policy will take effect. Effective dates must be reasonable. If your policy is calling for a revamp of existing policies, then a phase-in period may be needed. This phase-in period may range anywhere from a few months to a couple of years. A bill must carry an enforcement mechanism which states the penalty for noncompliance with the prescribed law and the agency responsible for the enforcement. Typically, this is done in Article IV. Article V calls for the nullification of existing policies in order to alleviate any conflict with the newly proposed policy action. Without enforcement, a bill is meaningless.

A copy of "A Bill to License Walk-In Medical Clinics" follows the standard format. You should compare the standard format with the specific example. Each major part of the example should correspond to the parts prescribed in the standard format.

Standard Format for a Bill

1	Article I:	State the new policy to be adopted in a brief
2		declarative sentence, or in as few sentences
3		as possible.
4	Article II:	Define any ambiguous terms inherent in
5		Article I.
6	Article III:	Indicate the implementation date.
7	Article IV:	Name the government agency that will
8		oversee the enforcement of the bill along with
9		the specific enforcement mechanism.
10	Article V:	State that all other laws that are in conflict
11		with this new policy shall hereby be declared
12		null and void.

Respectfully Submitted to
the Committee on (Public
Welfare, Foreign Affairs,
Economics)

(Signature)

Type Your Name
Type Your School Name

A Bill to License Walk-In Medical Clinics

1	Article I:	All private and public walk-in medical clinics
2		shall be subject to licensing by the federal
3		government.
4	Article II:	This federal licensing shall limit their medical
5		services to nonemergency or non–life-threatening
6		procedures.
7	Article III:	This bill shall take effect immediately upon
8		passage.
9	Article IV:	The Department of Health and Human Services will
10		oversee this licensing. Failure to comply will
11		result in the loss of license to operate.
12	Article V:	All laws in conflict with this bill will hereby
13		be declared null and void.

Respectfully Submitted
to the Committee on
Public Welfare

Maria Frye
Williams High School

There are several possible reasons for proposing legislation in bill form. First, a new law may be needed to solve a recently recognized problem. An example of such legislation was the Family Leave Bill, which was passed in 1992 by Congress and signed into law in 1993 by President Clinton. The bill would require companies with fifty or more employees to provide up to twelve weeks' unpaid leave of absence for the birth of a baby or other family emergencies. The legislation was most likely drafted to meet the demands placed upon the family when both parents are working.

A second reason for writing your topic as a bill may be the inadequacy of existing laws. The current college loan and scholarship controversy represents a topic that would fit this category. Present laws regarding payment of the borrowed money make it difficult to collect outstanding loans. A new proposal could call for the garnishing of wages once the student graduates and is gainfully employed.

Third, inconsistent policies may exist from state to state and a consistent policy may be needed at the federal level. At one time the drinking age in the United States differed from state to state. Some states allowed people to drink alcoholic beverages at age eighteen while other states required people to be twenty-one. In order to reduce the number of deaths and injuries that resulted from teenage drinking and driving, the federal government imposed a cut in federal highway funding to states that failed to increase their legal drinking age to twenty-one. This legislation brought about a uniformity in the legal drinking age across the country.

Resolutions address observed problems and make recommendations for improvement. Resolutions do not have the force of law; they urge action to deal with the problem without specifying exactly how the problem is to be solved. Congress, for example, can urge the executive branch to take a firmer stand on trade with Japan without saying which actions ought to be taken. Unlike bills, which include articles or sections, resolutions use "whereas" clauses. A standard format for writing an NFL resolution follows. This format lists the criteria for each whereas clause of a resolution. The whereas clauses provide the rationale for some action to be taken to solve a problem. Since the whereas clauses are interdependent, they flow as one long sentence connected by semicolons and the conjunction *and*.

Notice that the initial whereas clauses include a description of the problem. Subsequent whereas clauses describe the scope and the impact of the problem. The number of whereas clauses will vary depending on the number of concerns that need to be addressed to bring about a resolution of the problem. Following the whereas clauses, a resolution includes a call for action. This call for action is prefaced by the words: "Therefore, be it resolved by this Student Congress here assembled . . . ."

A copy of "A Resolution to Reorganize the Federal Emergency Management Agency (FEMA)" follows the standard format. Compare the generic resolution to the FEMA resolution.

Standard Format for a Resolution

1	Whereas:	State the current problem (this needs to be
2		accomplished in one brief sentence); and
3	Whereas:	Describe the scope of the problem cited in
4		the first whereas clause (this clause needs
5		to flow logically from the first); and

6	Whereas:	Explain the impact of or the harms perpetuated by
7		the current problem (once again, the clause
8		needs to flow in a logical sequence).
9	Therefore,	be it resolved by this Student Congress here
10		assembled that: state your recommendation for
11		dealing with the problem (the resolution should
12		be a clear call for action).

Respectfully Submitted to
the Committee on (Public
Welfare, Foreign Affairs,
Economics)

(Signature)

Type your name
Type your school name

A Resolution to Reorganize the Federal Emergency Management Agency (FEMA)

1	Whereas:	The Federal Emergency Management Agency
2		is not responding to recent natural-disaster
3		victims in an efficient and expedient manner;
4		and
5	Whereas:	This lack of efficiency and expediency has left
6		thousands of individuals without an adequate
7		supply of food, clothing, and shelter; and
8	Whereas:	This lack of supplies has fueled a public outcry
9		for change.
10	Therefore,	be it resolved by this Student Congress here
11		assembled that FEMA be reorganized to better
12		meet the needs of natural-disaster victims.

Respectfully Submitted
to the Committee on
Public Welfare

Daniel Jiu
Lincoln High School

Resolutions provide a "sense of the legislature." A resolution does not include a specific date for implementation or any enforcement mechanism. Congress could propose a resolution to the executive branch advising that no new laws are needed to reduce pollution if the consensus of the legislature is that current laws are sufficient and need only to be adequately enforced by the Environmental Protection Agency.

Additionally, the United States Congress may draft a resolution when it is unable to write a bill. For instance, the United States cannot pass a law that gives the United States jurisdiction over another country. Hence, a resolution (similar to actions taken by the United Nations) would be in order. An example of this might be the United States Congress pressuring the administration to convince Israel to relinquish the Golan Heights in return for guarantees to protect its security.

A copy of the resolution concerning trade with Japan debated in the Super Session of the National Forensic League's National Congress in June 1992 is included at the beginning of this book. This is an example of a topic that could be written as either a bill or a resolution. Congress could pass a bill to impose quotas on the number of Japanese automobiles imported into the United States or send a resolution to the administration to get tough in trade relations with Japan. It is our judgment that "A Resolution Concerning Japanese Trade" creates several problems that could be avoided by giving careful attention to the content and language of the whereas clauses. A revised version of the resolution follows:

A Resolution Concerning Japanese Trade

1	Whereas:	The United States had a $185 billion
2		balance-of-trade deficit with Japan
3		during the last fiscal year; and
4	Whereas:	This balance-of-payments deficit was
5		caused by unfair Japanese trade
6		policy; and
7	Whereas:	Japan's trade policy will continue
8		to employ unfair import taxes, licensing
9		procedures, and other practices to protect
10		its markets; and
11	Whereas:	These trade policies will result in
12		a continued balance-of-payments deficit
13		for the United States.

14	Therefore,	be it resolved by this Student Congress
15		here assembled that the U.S. should
16		implement trade policies similar to
17		those employed by Japan until a system
18		of fair trade between the two nations
19		can be negotiated.

Observe that the first whereas clause in the revised resolution is a clear statement of the problem and includes a time frame for the balance-of-payments deficit. In the original resolution we have no clear time referent for the $185 billion balance-of-payments deficit.[3] Unless both sides in the debate are operating from a clear understanding of the problem, muddled argument will result.

In the original resolution the second, third, and fourth whereas clauses contain assertions (undeveloped claims) that are better left to the debate itself. The revised version of the resolution sets up the conditions for debate to take place.

Notice that the second whereas clause attributes the problem to a trade policy Japan has in place and the third whereas clause makes specific the unfair practices that constitute Japanese trade policy. The fourth whereas clause makes it clear that Japan will continue to pursue these practices. The suggested course of action in the last ("Be it resolved") clause lets the executive branch of government know that the Congress wants action to be taken that will bring about fair trade. The exact actions are left to the executive branch.

Very careful attention to the content of the articles or whereas clauses in a bill or resolution will make it easier for participants to engage in productive debate. Careful attention to the language of a bill or resolution will prevent misunderstandings that arise when articles or whereas clauses contain ambiguous words or unclear referents. Instructors or coaches should assist students by carefully checking bills and resolutions before they are submitted for debate.

The National Forensic League classifies resolutions as simple, joint, or concurrent. A simple resolution is the most common. Usually, a simple resolution is a measure adopted by one chamber or legislative body. The National Forensic League defines a simple resolution as generalized statements expressing the belief of a group adopting them, and they do not have the force of law.[4] The U.S. House of Representatives (apart from the Senate) may adopt a resolution expressing its sentiment on an executive matter and offer recommendations to the president.

A joint resolution is one adopted by both the House of Representatives and the Senate. Most often it is used to deal with a single appropriation or to propose amendments to the Constitution.[5] Joint resolutions brought before the United States Congress require passage by both the House and the Senate before going to the president for signature.[6]

Concurrent resolutions must be adopted by both the House of Representatives and the Senate. Then, the resolution goes to the president for signing. This resolution does not carry the force of law. Congress may draft a concurrent resolution to coordinate budget decisions between both houses. Additionally, a concurrent resolution may be drafted when Congress wishes to express its sentiment on foreign policy or a domestic issue.[7] Joint and concurrent resolutions are rarely debated in Student Congress.

With a firm understanding of the distinctions between a resolution and a bill, you are ready to engage in the writing process. If you follow the procedures recommended in this chapter, your task should be easier.

Writing Legislation for Student Congress Competition

An initial consideration for Student Congress legislation is the suitability of topics for debate. A recent packet of twenty-five bills and resolutions received for an upcoming congress included the following: ''A Bill to Sterilize Children of Mothers Under the Age of Eighteen,'' ''A Bill to Castrate or Execute Repeat Sex Offenders,'' ''A Resolution to Repeal the Bill of Rights,'' and ''A Bill to Make the Moon the Fifty-First State.'' Some monitoring of legislation submitted for debate is necessary. There are many excellent topics that avoid the sensational or bizarre.

It is very important to use clear, concise language when writing legislation. So often bills and resolutions lack a sense of focus; what could have been stated in several succinct whereas clauses or articles seems to ramble on forever. Therefore, the need for concise expression is essential. Additionally, the language of a Student Congress bill or resolution must always be in the imperative mood, stating exactly what is to be done and by whom.

Also keep in mind your purpose for writing the bill or resolution. Ask yourself questions to define the primary objective prior to writing. For instance, why is this legislation being drafted? Is the topic really important? What will this legislation accomplish? What will be the impact of the legislation? Once you have answered these questions and have a clear understanding of the objective, you are ready to write the bill or resolution.

You are now ready to outline or prepare a rough draft of your legislation. Seek feedback from your teammates and instructor or coach before preparing a final draft. Remember to refer to the generic examples for writing an NFL bill or resolution that were presented earlier in this chapter. The examples will remind you of what is to be included in each article or whereas clause. Once you are satisfied that the necessary changes have been made, you are ready to prepare the final draft.

It is essential to type the final draft of the bill or resolution that you will submit for competition. Typewritten legislation is easy to read and allows for the distribution of copies to participating schools. Double spacing is a requirement for properly written legislation. Once again, the double-spaced document is easy to read and allows Student Congress representatives to easily amend the legislation in competition. The numbering of each double-spaced line will allow for speedy reference to a part of the legislation that may need amending.

After you have written your bill or resolution you *must* make a determination as to the committee to which you will submit your legislation. For simplicity's sake, Student Congress has only three committees: Public Welfare, Economics, and Foreign Affairs. Frequently, legislation will fit under more than one committee. For example, legislation that recommends aid to another country, although it may seem to fit under Foreign Affairs, may be more appropriately submitted to the Economics committee if the debate focuses on spending and appropriations. The example presented earlier in this chapter that called for European countries to assume a major part of the cost of NATO troops stationed there fits into this category. Although the legislation deals with the support of troops on foreign soil, the primary focus of the debate is an economic one. Hence, the legislation would be more appropriately submitted to the Committee on Economics.

Most often the topic of your bill or resolution will dictate the committee for submission. Legislation that safeguards the general well-being of the people would come under Public Welfare. Legislative issues related to spending, appropriations, tax incentives, and the like would fall under Economics. Finally, legislation dealing with the United States' relations with other countries would most likely come under Foreign Affairs. When in doubt, refer back to the key words that were helpful in locating information about the general topic area. Many times these terms will indicate the overall focus of the debate.

Summary

This chapter has attempted to provide you with sufficient information to prepare legislation for Student Congress competition. By following the guidelines presented, you should be able to locate controversial topics suitable for legislative debate. One way to accomplish this is to brainstorm a list of possible topics with your congress group. Once you have listed the topics, preliminary research will assist you in determining whether the topic will provide for good debate. The information you locate should also help you make a decision about whether the subject can best be treated as a bill or resolution. Finally, writing the legislation according to the recommended format will ensure that you include all of the relevant components.

A well-written bill or resolution is necessary for meaningful debate. Legislation that is properly drafted will provide a clear focus for both sides of a controversy. If the topic is current and significant, the debate will be interesting and productive.

Notes

1. J. W. Patterson and David Zarefsky, *Contemporary Debate* (Boston: Houghton Mifflin, 1983), 5.

2. Roe v. Wade, 410 U.S. 113, 93 S.Ct. 705, 35 L.Ed. 2d 147 (1973).

3. We used the $185 billion figure reported in the resolution. We did not verify the accuracy of the figure because no time frame is included in the resolution.

4. *Student Congress Manual* (Ripon, Wis.: National Forensic League, 1992), 1.

5. Ibid. (See the NFL *Student Congress Manual* for additional information on joint resolutions.)

6. Susan Kellam, ed., *Congressional Quarterly Almanac* (Congressional Quarterly Inc., 1992), 81-D.

7. *Student Congress Manual,* 1.

Discussion Questions

1. Discuss the following statement: Topics for bills and resolutions prepared for Student Congress competition must be significant and should provide a balance between pro and con positions.

2. Why is it important for bills or resolutions submitted for debate to have significant written material readily available to participants?

3. Discuss the following statement: Reasonable people accept the risk of future action only if there is a strong probability that the proposed action will be beneficial.

4. Why would it be preferable to write a resolution rather than a bill calling for Israel to move out of the Golan Heights?

5. Discuss why a "Bill to Sterilize Children of Mothers Under Eighteen" should or should not be submitted for debate at a Student Congress.

6. Discuss the following statement: Limiting Student Congress bills and resolutions to the three topic areas—economics, public welfare, and foreign affairs—is a disservice to student participants.

7. When is it permissible to use the same topic area for a bill or resolution as has been recently debated at a Student Congress competition?

8. Why should you apply a stock issues analysis to a topic before you write a bill or resolution?

9. Why should a legislative body vote against a bill or resolution if the pro side fails to establish all four stock issues?

10. Discuss the differences in format and purposes between a bill and a resolution.

CHAPTER 5

Preparing Student Congress Speeches

Integral to the Student Congress process is the legislative speech. This persuasive speech is presented either in favor of or against the legislation being debated and is typically extemporaneous.

All legislative speeches should be tightly organized, with a brief introduction, clearly stated arguments that are supported with quality evidence, and a conclusion that emphasizes the impact of the arguments on the outcome of the bill or resolution. Three types of legislative speeches will be discussed in this chapter:

- the authorship speech;

- the con speech;

- the pro speech.

Additionally, the chapter will discuss the question-and-answer period that follows each of these speeches during the legislative session. A brief discussion of a speech supporting an amendment to a bill or resolution will be presented.

The Authorship Speech

The authorship speech is prepared and presented by the author of the legislation being debated. The speech should be a well-drafted manuscript speech with the qualities of an oration. This speech should be prepared well in advance of the competition and must include all of the compelling arguments in favor of the bill or resolution. Before preparing the authorship speech it is important to locate answers to the following questions: What is the objective of the bill or resolution? Why is the bill or resolution good policy? Will the benefits of the bill or resolution outweigh the disadvantages? What are the issues that must be developed to justify the legislation? What are the best arguments that can be developed to support these issues? How can the speech be organized to have the greatest impact? The answers to these questions will make it possible to develop an excellent authorship speech.

Because the authorship speech initiates the debate, it is essential that the major lines of analysis in support of the legislation be clearly formulated. A well-organized speech provides the framework for the debate. Judges and student participants flow the issues and arguments and formulate responses either in favor of or against each major line of analysis presented. (See Chapter Two.)

It is our judgment that the authorship speech that initiates the debate on ''A Resolution Concerning Trade with Japan'' (see Chapter One) has several weaknesses. First, the two major lines of analysis presented in the opening speech discuss the poor relationship Americans have with the Japanese and indicate that Americans are upset with this relationship. These two arguments are really the same. Two issues that are crucial to the debate—the impact of the balance-of-trade deficit on the United States' economy and the causes of the significant imbalance of trade—are not developed. Hence, important issues that might have set the foundation for arguments in succeeding speeches go undiscussed until much later in the debate. This poses a serious problem. A well-organized authorship speech that sets out all major issues is critical to the success of legislative debates. We acknowledge that this deficiency in the debate on ''A Resolution Concerning Trade with Japan'' may be attributed to the fact that an individual other than the author presented the speech in the Super Session of the NFL National Congress. The author of the legislation probably would have developed and presented a persuasive speech including these significant issues.

The major lines of analysis that are crucial to the advocacy of the legislation need to be identified in outline form before writing the speech. These lines of analysis will be discovered by asking the questions posed above and by doing the necessary research to uncover relevant information on the topic. The nature of the topic will dictate the major relevant issues. The careful signposting of each major line of analysis will help student participants readily grasp and understand the issues crucial to the outcome of the debate.

Once you have identified the major issues in outline form you are ready to find subordinate arguments that support each issue. List as many subordinate arguments as possible. For instance, if you are advancing the argument that a protectionist trade policy will best serve America's interests, several subordinate arguments may be: such a policy will safeguard U.S. industries; it will save U.S. jobs; it will decrease our balance-of-trade deficit; and it will improve the American economy. You should be able to locate several good pieces of evidence to support each argument. Finally, you should choose the best evidence and the most convincing arguments to support each major line of analysis. (See Chapter Three.)

In order to ensure a clear and convincing delivery of the authorship speech and other legislative speeches, the following organizational format should be employed:

I. Introduction (assembled after the
   identification and the development
   of the major lines of analysis)
   A. Attention-getting device
   B. Statement of overall position
   C. Provide major lines of analysis
      (map direction of speech).

II. Body of speech
   A. First major line of analysis
      1. subordinate argument (with evidence)
      2. subordinate argument (with evidence)
   B. Second major line of analysis
      1. subordinate argument (with evidence)
      2. subordinate argument (with evidence)
   C. Third major line of analysis
      1. subordinate argument (with evidence)
      2. subordinate argument (with evidence)

III. Conclusion
   A. Recap major lines of analysis.
   B. Call for passage of legislation.

Not only is it important to provide a clear structure, but it is also crucial to provide documentation for the evidence used to support each argument. For example, if the authorship speech in the debate on "A Resolution Concerning Trade with Japan" had included documentation for the $185 billion balance-of-trade deficit, the resulting confusion could have been avoided. At a minimum, the documentation should include the source and a date. More complete documentation is preferable. It is also important to explain how the evidence warrants your conclusion and to show how the arguments relate back to your overall position. A sample authorship speech appears at the end of this chapter. Refer to it as needed.

The presentation of the authorship speech and other legislative speeches is as important as the preparation. Because the authorship speech is the only presentation prepared in advance of the actual debate, a manuscript may be employed. The author should be familiar enough with this document so the speech can be delivered extemporaneously.

Index cards are recommended for the delivery of the subsequent pro and con speeches. Notecards, when combined with eye contact and facial expression, allow for a more direct delivery of the legislative speech. Eye contact with the audience and critic judges is essential. Audiences provide immediate feedback to the speaker. They will let you know if they understand your arguments, if they agree or disagree with the position you are taking in the debate, and if you are failing to communicate with them. It is virtually impossible to adapt to your audience if you are not looking at them and ''reading'' their reactions.

Additionally, the use of gestures will enhance your presentation and help emphasize different parts of your speech. Gestures should be natural and made from the shoulders using the entire arm. Remember to only use gestures that are meaningful and distinctive. Another important aspect of delivery is movement. In order to signpost your major lines of analysis, a step forward or a step to the right or left will reinforce the transitions you are making from one idea to another. Use of the aforementioned procedures will help you become a more effective debater.

Vocal warm-ups (for example, stretches, tongue-twisters, and the like) should be performed prior to competition. These will assist you in becoming a more articulate and more fluent speaker.

Personal appearance is another important facet of speech and debate. Imagine attending a lecture where the audience is better dressed than the keynote speaker. Careful attention should be paid to physical appearance. Student Congress participants should wear well-fitting clothing. There are few things more annoying than a speaker who is constantly tugging and adjusting his or her clothes. Moreover, jackets and ties are recommended for men and dresses for women. A participant should wear clothing that is appropriate for semi-formal gatherings.

Student Congress participants should take every opportunity available to speak in front of audiences. Speak often in classes, at meetings, and in practice congresses. The more often you speak, the more proficient you become. Fluency, eye contact, and your ability to overcome communication apprehension should improve.

The Con Speech

The primary purpose of the con speech is to provide issues, arguments, and evidence to defeat the bill or resolution. This involves presenting both constructive con arguments and refutation of pro positions. The first con speech should carefully lay out all the major positions the negative will be advocating, similar to the authorship speech that sets forth all the major arguments in favor of the legislation. It is especially important to raise any major issue that the authorship speech neglects.

In order to effectively refute and rebuild arguments, chamber participants must listen carefully to all preceding speeches, both pro and con. While listening, all participants need to maintain a flow chart of the arguments presented by previous speakers. (See Chapter Two.) In addition to flowing the arguments, a student participant wishing to address the chamber should write responses that indicate agreement or disagreement in a column next to the recorded arguments on the flow sheet. This will help speakers to advance the debate rather than merely repeat arguments that have already been presented. Speakers can advance the debate in a number of ways. First, they can offer new evidence to refute an argument directly or extend a previously presented argument that needs additional support. Additionally, new insights may be presented to enlighten the chamber participants about a perspective they may not have considered. Students wanting to present a con speech should be familiar with the research packets that they and their teammates developed. These packets will contain the best evidence available to refute the previous speaker's arguments or to support new arguments. Remember, all speeches will be more successful if they are clearly organized and delivered effectively.

The con speech should be structured according to the organizational pattern recommended in our discussion of authorship speeches and the same performance techniques should be applied.

The Pro Speech

Pro speeches that follow the authorship speech have the same ultimate goal: to advocate passage of the bill or resolution. One major difference is that successive pro speeches are not prepared manuscripts but are adapted to the flow of the debate. The objective of the pro speech is to rebuild arguments that have been attacked, to refute con arguments, and to extend the arguments presented in the authorship speech. The advice given for developing, organizing, and presenting con speeches is applicable.

The Question-and-Answer Period

In the aftermath of each legislative speech a question-and-answer period is conducted. There are several reasons for holding this question-and-answer period. First, it helps to clarify issues presented in both the pro and con speeches. Second, it helps to set up arguments that will be presented in subsequent speeches. Third, it helps to determine weak arguments that can be attacked later during the debate. Unlike cross-examination in academic debate or judicial courtroom proceedings, the question-and-answer period does not allow one individual to ask multiple questions. Therefore, questions must be carefully phrased in order to obtain the desired response. Student participants should not ask questions solely for the purpose of securing participation points from the critic judge. Student Congress participants should only ask questions that are relevant and meaningful to the legislative debate. Additionally, the participants asking the questions should not engage in cross-debate with the speaker but should only seek answers to their questions that will be used to structure arguments in succeeding speeches.

The question-and-answer period is overseen by the presiding officer. A participant wanting to ask a question must first be recognized by the chair. If a question is strictly for a point of information and requires only one question, the participant simply asks the question. On the other hand, if the question is more complex and involves two parts, the participant must preface the question with the following: ''Will the representative submit to a two-part question?'' If the speaker agrees, the participant can proceed with the questioning. A question that supports the speaker's position is called a friendly question. If a participant chooses to advance the speaker's cause it is done by asking: ''Will the representative yield to a friendly question?'' prior to asking the question. Finally, if a representative wants to ask a follow-up question right after a first question, he or she should immediately stand and address the chair with: ''Will the representative yield to a follow-up question?'' Participants may not ask a question without permission of the chair and the speaker.

Various types of questions can be asked in order to move the debate along. Questions that challenge the source of the information may indicate specific biases. Questions that cast doubt on the ability of a particular policy enforcement mechanism can establish a circumvention argument. Questions pointing out inconsistencies and weaknesses in argumentation may also be used. For example, in the authorship speech on ''A Resolution Concerning Trade with Japan'' the speaker claims that our balance-of-trade deficit with Japan is $185 billion (he offers no time frame). Later in the debate a speaker states that the balance-of-trade deficit with Japan is $4 billion. A key question to ask the speaker in the aftermath of this speech would be: "What is the specific time frame for the $185 billion balance-of-trade deficit and the $4 billion balance-of-trade deficit?" Or, "Two very different balance-of-trade figures have been introduced. Which is the correct amount?" Both of these questions would be crucial to the debate and to voting on legislation that requires protectionist policies.

Speakers answering the questions need to be well versed in the topic. Not only should they demonstrate a command of the subject when speaking, but their expertise should be evident when responses are provided during the question-and-answer period.

A few strategies can be used by speakers when they are uncertain about answering questions. Think carefully before you respond to a question. Answer the question truthfully, but avoid giving your opponents information that could conceivably weaken your overall position. Provide only what the question requires. Refrain from giving misinformation; never mislead. Provide only information that advances the legislative debate. Do not hesitate to ask the questioner to rephrase the question if it is unclear or if you are unsure of what information is being sought. This allows additional time to think about your answer and precludes giving information not requested. Paying close attention to the questions and the answers may suggest arguments that need to be refuted or reestablished.

The Amendment Speech

Amendments are not frequently offered in Student Congress. However, when an amendment to a bill or resolution is proposed, the author has the responsibility to explain the import of the change. At a minimum the amendment speech should include a statement about the purpose of the proposed change. If you can specify why the change will result in better debate, you should provide this information. This speech will probably determine whether the amendment will be accepted or rejected.

A Sample Authorship Speech

The following is a student-written authorship speech prepared to support Bill 303, "A Bill to Restrict Japanese Automobile Imports."

Politicians and economists are finally recognizing what the American public has known for some time—we are in a recession. Stores and restaurants are without customers, problems of severe unemployment and increased costs of unemployment compensation and welfare are delivering a staggering blow to our economy.

To rectify this problem, Bill 303 requires that the United States reduce Japanese automobile imports by 15 percent over the next five years. I ask your support for this bill for the following three reasons:

1. Bill 303 will fuel our economy.

2. New jobs will be created.

3. The federal deficit will be reduced.

First, Bill 303 will stimulate the American economy. This action will bring about an end to the recession and the suffering we are experiencing because of slow economic growth. Bill 303 will accomplish this by decreasing the competition in the automobile industry. Any concern about the impact of Bill 303 on Japan is not warranted. According to the February 10, 1992, issue of *Time* magazine, Japan has "a powerful, dynamic economy which could overtake the United States in the year 2000." By decreasing the number of Japanese cars allowed into the United States, the United States automobile market will benefit. Reducing imports will provide an incentive to buy American-made cars, which will stimulate significant growth in related industries such as rubber, steel, plastics, and electronics.

My second line of analysis is that jobs will be created. The unemployment rate at the end of 1991 was very high. According to the February 3, 1992, issue of *Newsweek*, 6.8 percent of the population over the age of sixteen was unemployed. Major employers such as General Electric, Phillips Petroleum, and IBM have announced major cutbacks in their work force and economists are predicting that this is only the beginning of massive layoffs throughout the economy. The problem facing the unemployed is that there are few jobs being created and they have nowhere to turn. Companies are struggling to survive and cannot afford to increase their work force.

If we decrease automobile imports as called for in Bill 303, we will create new and well-paid jobs for the unemployed. The auto industry provides a variety of jobs from manufacturing to sales directly and indirectly in related industries. As confidence in the American economy grows, spending will increase and more and more jobs will be created.

My third line of analysis is that the federal deficit will decrease. Currently the deficit is approximately three trillion dollars and growing. Americans spend billions of dollars on Japanese cars each year. By decreasing Japanese automobile imports the sale of American-made cars will increase and our economy will be revitalized. Fewer unemployed workers means more revenue for the government and the cost of unemployment and welfare benefits will decline. In a January issue of *Forbes,* an auto analyst stated that Europe has already limited Japanese auto imports to 8 percent of their total market. I believe that it is wise for the United States to take action now to limit Japanese imports.

I ask you to vote for Bill 303 to save America from a continuing and devastating recession. This bill will stimulate the economy, create numerous jobs, and cut the outlay of government funds for social services. Ultimately, the size of the federal deficit will be brought under control. We can accomplish this by phasing in a 15 percent cut in Japanese automobiles over a five-year period without causing undue economic hardships for Japan.

Summary

Persuading members of a legislative body to vote for the position you advocate is the ultimate test of success in Student Congress competition. Since the opportunity to speak is limited, it is vital that your speech be skillfully crafted and delivered. Constant practice is required for success.

Because you are limited to three or four minutes' speaking time, it is essential that you organize your remarks to have the greatest possible impact. Arguments must be stated in clear, concise language and supporting evidence must be carefully selected and documented. Pay careful attention to your audience as you speak, and adapt as necessary. Your delivery should be natural and forceful.

The authorship speech and the first con speech are especially important in Student Congress debate. The authorship speech provides the framework for the debate by providing all major lines of argument to be advanced in favor of the bill or resolution. The first con speech provides an opportunity for those in the opposition to set forth all major negative positions. If these two speeches succeed, the debate that follows is more likely to stay focused. All succeeding speeches in a congressional debate should move the debate forward. Refuting your opponent's arguments and rebuilding your own arguments are essential.

Use the question-and-answer period to your advantage. Carefully worded questions can gain admissions that can be used to weaken an opponent's position or strengthen your own. The successful participant in Student Congress is one who listens carefully and flows the debate, including the question-and-answer period, from the beginning of the debate until the final vote is completed.

Discussion Questions

1. Explain why the authorship speech should include all major issues in support of the bill or resolution.

2. Discuss the factors that go into deciding which arguments and how many arguments to include as support for each major issue.

3. Why should all congress speeches except the authorship speech be delivered from limited notes?

4. Why is it important to include complete documentation, including the date, for evidence used in a legislative debate?

5. Why is maintaining eye contact with the audience and critic judges crucial to effective debating?

6. Why should the first con speech include a negative constructive position for each major issue that the con side will likely debate?

7. Why are critical listening and flowing arguments necessary for effective participation in Student Congress?

8. Why is it important for every congress speech to be carefully organized, with major arguments stated clearly and concisely?

9. Discuss why the question-and-answer period is important in Student Congress debates.

CHAPTER 6

The Mechanics of Student Congress

Chapters One through Five provide the foundation for successful participation in legislative debate. Equipped with the knowledge of how arguments function in a legislative assembly, you are now ready to engage in the give-and-take of Student Congress competition.

Student Congress tournaments are hosted by many schools across the nation, especially by the members of the National Forensic League. These schools usually accept the basic guidelines established by the NFL executive council, which appear in the NFL *Student Congress Manual*. This chapter will focus on Student Congress debate, highlighting the procedures used by a majority of host schools. Six specific areas will be covered:

- committee meetings and legislative sessions
- presiding officer responsibilities
- parliamentary procedure
- critic judge responsibilities
- Student Congress politics
- voting procedures

Committee Meetings and Legislative Sessions

Most Student Congress competitions convene for one to two days (the duration may vary from one region of the country to another). When you arrive at the host school and register with the tournament manager, your school will receive a registration packet that will include a schedule of events, committee assignments, judging assignments, and legislative-chamber assignments for all student participants. Legislative chambers are composed of a cross section of students from participating schools. Most often the number of students assigned to a chamber ranges anywhere from twenty-five to thirty. Chambers can be apportioned to include members of like experience and ability or members with a range of experience and ability. A mixture of different abilities helps to provide role models for the beginners, while homogenous grouping provides for debate among participants of near equal ability. Legislative-chamber assignments are usually prepared beforehand by the tournament coordinators (the number of chambers varies according to the number of students entered). Chamber assignments include committee appointments. (See Appendices for an example of chamber rosters with committee appointments.) After registration, the first order of business is the committee meeting, followed by the legislative sessions. The meeting and the sessions provide an opportunity for students to engage in two deliberative, decision-making settings.

Student Congress, following the precedent set by the NFL, uses only three committee designations: Public Welfare, Foreign Affairs, and Economics. Prior to legislative debate sessions, student-written legislation is submitted to these committees for scrutiny by competitors. Participating schools are usually mailed a packet of legislation several weeks prior to the competition. Most often, this legislation is numbered, which denotes its committee assignment. For example, the 100s may denote Public Welfare bills and resolutions; the 200s, Foreign Affairs; and the 300s, Economics. These committees rank the three or four pieces of legislation deemed most suitable for debate. Only bills and resolutions reported out of committee meetings are debated.

If your school delegation is large enough, there will be one or more persons represented on each committee. Committee chairpersons are either assigned by the tournament staff or elected in committee. The chairperson should be capable of leading the members towards a consensus on the best legislation. Although most Student Congress participants wish to report out legislation from their own school, it is more important

to release legislation that meets the requirements of a good bill/resolution (discussed in Chapter Four). At a minimum, the bill/resolution should be current and controversial and provide for well-balanced debate.

Although a number of students from one school may be represented on a given committee, only one vote is allowed per school to alleviate favoritism during the selection process. After the committee makes its choices, the chairperson reports the rank-ordered legislation to the tournament tabulation room for posting. The first ranked bill or resolution from each committee is debated before the second ranked bill or resolution. The legislative chambers then convene for debate. Invitational Student Congresses usually schedule two or three legislative sessions, depending on the host school, league rules, and so forth. A typical session will run 2½ to 3 hours, and each bill or resolution released by committee will be debated for approximately one hour (NFL Student Congress rules and other league rules may allow for time extensions). State and national tournaments may have more sessions and different time constraints.

Our discussion will be limited to the two-day format, which incorporates three legislative sessions. Most often the first session is scheduled on Friday evening immediately after the committee meetings or the dinner break. This first session runs longer than the second and third sessions in order to conduct preliminary business. For example, the election of presiding officers for each of the three sessions is conducted. Students who wish to run for presiding officer are nominated by their peers. Nominees are given time to tell the chamber why they are qualified to oversee a legislative session. The chamber votes after the brief speeches are finished. Candidates select the session they wish to chair based on the number of votes they receive (i.e., the most votes, first choice; next highest votes, second choice; and so forth). While the presiding officer election is taking place, a seating chart is circulated for each participant to include his or her name and school in the appropriate box. Care should be taken to legibly write the names and match the box on the chart with the correct seat. The seating chart is used by the presiding officer and the critic judges to identify the participants.

The second and third sessions are usually scheduled for Saturday morning and afternoon, respectively. A standard Student Congress schedule of events appears below. Notice the placement of committee meetings and legislative sessions. Spacing the sessions over two days allows for better debate on more issues.

Student Congress Schedule of Events

Friday

Registration	4:00 p.m.–4:30 p.m.
Committee Meetings	4:30 p.m.–5:15 p.m.
Dinner Break	5:15 p.m.–6:00 p.m.
Session I	6:00 p.m.–8:45 p.m.

Saturday

Session II	8:30 a.m.–11:00 a.m.
Lunch	11:00 a.m.–12:00 noon
Session III	12:00 noon–2:30 p.m.
Elections	2:40 p.m.–3:00 p.m.
Awards	3:30 p.m.–4:00 p.m.

All three sessions follow a similar order of business. (See Order of Business agenda below.) First, the presiding officer calls the session to order and issues parliamentary rules or comments on how the chamber will be run. Next, the presiding officer will call for the main motion to open the debate on the first bill/resolution. The legislative debate begins with a call for a four-minute authorship speech followed by a two-minute question-and-answer period. The authorship speech is followed by the first con speech, which is usually four minutes in length and another two-minute question-and-answer period. Alternating speeches, pro and con, are presented until the debate is concluded. The pro and con speeches are typically three minutes long and are followed by a one-minute question-and-answer period. The presiding officer may call for motions during the debate after a pair of speeches has been presented. A vote to pass or defeat the legislation is taken at the end of the hour-long debate. Usually a five-minute recess is taken and then the next piece of legislation is debated.

Order of Business for Student Congress

1. Invocation

2. Call to order

3. Roll call of members and confirmation

4. Special orders
   a. Review of special rules
   b. Review of Student Congress procedures
   c. Special announcements and questions

5. Consideration of calendar

6. Election of presiding officer [may occur prior to the call to order]

7. Committee meetings [may be held at a time prearranged by the tournament coordinators prior to the first session]

8. Floor debate on bills/resolutions

9. Selection of outstanding and superior Student Congress participants

10. Award of congress gavels and plaques[1]

Presiding Officer Responsibilities

Anyone who participates in Student Congress may choose to run for presiding officer. The presiding officer is responsible for conducting business during the legislative session and ensuring that the session runs smoothly. The skills needed to succeed in this position include a command of parliamentary procedure, the ability to maintain order, and the ability to follow established rules and guidelines and to enforce them uniformly. The presiding officer needs to keep an accurate record of legislative participation in order to give each member an equal opportunity to speak. The presiding officer times speeches and question-and-answer periods. A list of additional presiding officer guidelines follows later in this chapter.

Once nominated, the candidates for presiding officer will be allotted thirty seconds to tell the chamber why they are the best person for the position. Candidates usually stress their past experience and they try to convince the chamber that they will be fair and impartial. Most often, students are looking for a presiding officer who is knowledgeable, well organized, prepared, and impartial.

To succeed, the presiding officer must understand the basic principles of parliamentary procedure. A copy of the NFL's Table of Most Frequently Used Parliamentary Motions appears later in this chapter. Understanding how to utilize these motions effectively will provide for the smooth flow of business.

Maintaining a record of the flow of business is the best way for the presiding officer to ensure accuracy and efficiency. Since the session commences with an authorship speech followed by a brief question-and-answer period, the first con speech, and so on, this information can be recorded in an abbreviated form. For example, write in descending order: A, Q&A, CON #1, Q&A, PRO #1, Q&A, CON #2, Q&A, PRO #2, and so forth. Enter the time next to each abbreviation. As each part of the legislative debate occurs, cross out the letter which it represents. This will prevent confusion, and the presiding officer will know the amount of time remaining for debate. The record with corresponding times should be kept independent of the seating chart that indicates member participation.

The following is a modification of presiding officer guidelines recommended by the Northern Illinois Student Congress coaches.

Recommended Guidelines for Presiding Officer

1. Commence session with polite, firm, and direct statements that establish your authority. (Use a gavel to call the meeting to order.) Some suggestions:
   (a) Establish whether student participants need to ask permission to leave or enter the chamber.

    (b) Determine the status of the debate and occasionally announce how much progress has been made and how much time remains for debate.

    (c) Set the ground rules for when motions will be allowed.

    (d) Inform student participants that you will stop them when their speaking time has elapsed.

2. Maintain a careful record of those who have spoken and have asked and answered questions. Recognize individuals who have been less involved than others.

3. Encourage participation.

4. Be attuned to the needs of your representatives. Provide them with an accurate account of what's happening as necessary.

5. Stand to count the vote.

6. Maximize debate. Discourage student participants from playing parliamentary games.

7. Overcome acts of favoritism.

8. Keep order. Humor is fine, but do not overuse it.

9. Control the clock. Avoid being too slow when recognizing individuals. Stop the clock during question-and-answer periods when reading the seating chart. Otherwise, let the clock run during the questions and answers.

Parliamentary Procedure

Student Congress legislative sessions are governed by the basic principles of parliamentary procedure. We recommend using *Robert's Rules of Order*.[2] There are five reasons for using parliamentary procedure:

- to provide equity to all members
- to consider one item at a time
- to expedite business
- to safeguard the voice of the minority
- to ensure the decision of the majority

It is important for all Student Congress participants to have a fundamental understanding of parliamentary procedure and Student Congress guidelines. First, the presiding officer (referred to as the chair) calls the legislative session to order. Next, the chair addresses the first order of business that opens debate. All legislative business is conducted through the presiding officer. Any congress participant wanting to secure the floor during a debate must do so through the chair. Most often, this is accomplished by rising, addressing the chair ("Mr./Madame Chair"), and being recognized by the chair. Once recognized, the member introduces business in the form of a motion ("I move"). Several motions require a second and are open to debate (see Table). Next, the chair calls for an immediate vote on the business at hand. The chair asks all members in favor of the motion to vote, followed by a call for a negative vote, and then a call for abstentions. The result of the vote is announced.

Several basic rules of debate apply when using parliamentary procedure. First, each member is entitled to speak once on a question. Sometimes a member can speak twice or more on a particular question if everyone who wants to speak has been given an opportunity. When considering prospective speakers, the chair should remain neutral. Second, all inquiries are conducted through the chair. Finally, the maker of a motion typically has the privilege of opening and closing the debate. These guidelines are necessary to maintain a smooth-running session. Under no circumstances should parliamentary procedure be used frivolously. Filibustering, which is used in the United States Congress to deny others an opportunity to speak and put off a vote on a particular piece of legislation, is not allowed in Student Congress. All parliamentary maneuvers should enhance the debate and provide each student participant with a sound educational experience.

Parliamentary Procedure makes use of four Parliamentary Motions: main, subsidiary, incidental, and privileged. The National Forensic League recommends that students have a command of the most frequently used motions to ensure the smooth running of business.[3] The *main motion* is the most commonly used motion in Student Congress. It is used to introduce new business. For example, a motion to open debate on "A Resolution Concerning Trade with Japan" would be introduced with the words "I move to discuss Legislation F: A Resolution Concerning Trade with Japan." A main motion requires a second (a majority vote of the chamber).

Three of the more frequently used *subsidiary motions* are to amend, to table, and to extend debate. For example, to amend Resolution F, a speaker would say, "I move the amendment before you [proposed amendments must be submitted to the chair in written form before the actual motion is made] to add to line 1 of Resolution F between the terms 'a' and 'trade' the terms: '1991 fiscal year.' " Subsidiary motions require a second and are open to debate.

Incidental motions should be used sparingly. Incidental motions attempt to correct for errors and adjust for any digressions during the legislative debate. For instance, if the chair has made an error in recording the vote, a member may appeal the decision of the chair. This is done by stating: "Mr./Madame Chair, I would like to ask for a recount of the vote on the passage of Resolution F." Only three of the possible seven incidental motions require a second and none are open to debate. The critic judges need to ensure that the use of such motions is not detrimental to the educational process.

Finally, *privileged motions* are most often used to call the session to order or to adjourn. Several require a second and can be amended prior to a vote, e.g., "I move to adjourn until 1:00 p.m." A table from the NFL *Student Congress Manual* that includes the four types of motions with their order of precedence has been reprinted on pages 116–17. The chart is a helpful tool for all participants, especially the presiding officer, because it indicates the purpose of the motion, whether the motion needs a second, whether the motion is debatable, whether an amendment can be made, and whether the motion can interrupt the flow of the debate.

Critic Judge Responsibilities

In most cases two critic judges are assigned for each legislative chamber. This number may vary at an NFL district tournament or at the NFL National Speech Tournament. At the national tournament an adult parliamentarian and scorekeeper are used. Usually the coaches or assistant coaches representing the participating schools make up the judging pool. The most important function of the critic judge is to assess the student's proficiency as a legislative debater. This includes the student's ability to present well-developed constructive arguments in support of or in opposition to the legislation. Not only should the debaters present well-developed refutations but they should extend arguments as well. This can be accomplished through the direct refutation of the previous speaker's arguments (see Chapter Two).

Table of Most Frequently Used Parliamentary Motions
Adapted for use in NFL Student Congresses

Type	Motion	Purpose	Second Required?	Debatable?	Amendable?	Required Vote	May Interrupt a Speaker
Privileged	24. Fix Time for Reassembling	To arrange time of next meeting	Yes	Yes-T	Yes-T	Majority	Yes
	23. Adjourn	To dismiss the meeting	Yes	No	Yes-T	Majority	No
	22. To Recess	To dismiss the meeting for a specific length of time	Yes	Yes	Yes-T	Majority	No
	21. Rise to a Question of Privilege	To make a personal request during debate	No	No	No	Decision of Chair	Yes
	20. Call for the Orders of the Day	To force consideration of a postponed motion	No	No	No	Decision of Chair	Yes
Incidental	19. Appeal a Decision of the Chair	To reverse the decision of the chairman	Yes	No	No	Majority	Yes
	18. Rise to a Point of Order or Parliamentary Procedure	To correct a parliamentary error or ask a question	No	No	No	Decision of Chair	Yes
	17. Division of the Chamber	To verify a voice vote	No	No	No	Decision of Chair	Yes
	16. Object to the Consideration of a Question	To suppress action	No	No	No	Decision of Chair	Yes
	15. To Divide a Motion	To consider its parts separately	Yes	No	No	2/3	Yes
	14. Leave to Modify or Withdraw a Motion	To modify or withdraw a motion	No	No	Yes	Majority	No
	13. To Suspend the Rules	To take action contrary to standing rules	Yes	No	No	2/3	No

	Motion	Purpose					
Subsidiary	12. To Rescind	To repeal previous action	Yes	Yes	Yes	2/3	No
	11. To Reconsider	To consider a defeated motion again	Yes	Yes	No	Majority	No
	10. To Take from the Table	To consider tabled motion	Yes	No	No	Majority	No
	9. To Lay on the Table	To defer action	Yes	No	No	Majority	No
	8. Previous Question	To force an immediate vote	Yes	No	No	2/3	No
	7. To Limit or Extend Debate	To modify freedom of debate	Yes	Yes	Yes-T	2/3	No
	6. To Postpone to a Certain Time	To defer action	Yes	Yes	Yes	Majority	Yes
	5. To Refer to a Committee*	For further study	Yes	Yes	Yes	Majority	Yes
	4. To Amend an Amendment*	To modify an amendment	1/3	Yes	No	Majority	No
	3. To Amend*	To modify a motion	1/3	Yes	Yes	Majority	No
	2. To Postpone Indefinitely	To suppress action	Yes	Yes	No	Majority	No
Main	1. Main Motion	To introduce a business	Yes	Yes	Yes	Majority	No

T—Time

*Nos. 3 and 4 by:
1. Adding (Inserting)
2. Striking Out (Deleting)
3. Substituting

*No. 5 Should Include:
1. How Appointed?
2. The Number
3. Report When?
    or
To What Standing Committee

The only way the judge can make this assessment is by making a detailed flow chart of the arguments. The flow will assist the judge in determining which member is the best debater. The judge uses one of several possible critique sheets (see Appendix) to record comments about the speaker's performance. Typically, the sheets provide a continuum for rating an individual's presentation. Two judges alternate in the assessment of speakers, to allow time for writing the critique. Any judge affiliated with a particular school should decline to critique his or her own debaters. In addition to rating the speakers, the critic judge is responsible for noting and recording each member's participation. This allows credit for motions made, questions asked and answers provided, and amendments proposed.

Critique sheets are collected periodically throughout the session and brought to the tabulation room for recording. At the end of the legislative session the judges confer to decide on participation points for each member and record the points on a seating chart. Additionally, the judges are responsible for nominating two or three individuals (according to local customs and/or rules) who they believe performed best during the session.

In addition to awarding points to the participants, the judges assess the performance of the presiding officer. Once again, a critique sheet similar to the sheets used in assessing the member's performance is used. The presiding officer can be awarded up to twelve points. Although alternate methods for scoring the presiding officer's performance exist, the assessment of the presiding officer should be based on the criteria mentioned earlier in this chapter.

Nomination of the best speakers takes place at the end of each legislative session. Best presiding officer nominations take place at the end of the final legislative session. Individual judges are responsible for nominating a member from each session for best speaker and mutually agree upon the best presiding officer. Nomination forms are included in the folder containing seating charts, and critique forms are placed in the chamber at the beginning of each legislative session. The students eventually vote for the best speakers and presiding officers from the judges' list of nominees. This process will be explained later in this chapter.

Student Congress Politics

Student Congress is distinct from the other interscholastic speech events because it allows the students to decide ultimately who receives the most awards. This has a great impact on what happens in the chamber. School participants usually engage in a kind of politics similar to the partisan politics of our U.S. Congress. For instance, students from one school delegation may ally with another school delegation to form a voting bloc, or a student from one school may ask a student participant from another school to vote for their resolution or bill as best legislation in exchange for a vote for one of their delegates as best presiding officer.

Recommended guidelines for Student Congress politics follow. The list provides a number of helpful hints that you should practice in competition.

Recommended Guidelines for Student Congress Politics

1. Be courteous to all coaches and student participants.

2. Refrain from being overly polite. Insincere behavior is easily detected by fellow representatives.

3. Attempt to form your own voting coalitions. Be aware of voting coalitions that are in direct opposition to your voting bloc.

4. Take notice of school voting patterns. Prior notice will help you alter voting patterns to your advantage.

5. Engage in casual discussion with other students before the legislative session. This will increase your opportunities to assume a prominent position in the legislative session.

6. Do not underestimate the power of politics; if you play the game, results may turn in your favor.

7. Refrain from "ad hominem" argument (attacking the person rather than the issue).

8. Limit the use of parliamentary motions. Overuse may detract from the debate and diminish votes.

9. Recognize the needs of fellow representatives and respond accordingly.

10. Practice the ten-mile rule. Refrain from talking about tournament events during the competition. It is wise to wait until you have returned to your school to evaluate the congress.

It is necessary for student delegates to realize the importance of Student Congress politics and the impact it has on the outcome of the competition.

Voting Procedures

As mentioned earlier in this chapter, Student Congress is unique because students decide who will receive most of the awards. Awards are given in several categories: best legislation, best presiding officer, outstanding speaker, and superior speaker. The Outstanding Speaker Award is given to the top speaker in each chamber, followed by the Superior Speaker Award to the next-best speaker. A Critic's Choice Award is determined by the adult judges. Usually the speaker with the most points in each chamber is given the Critic's Choice Award. A Sweepstakes Award is presented at some invitational congresses to the school that has the best overall record. Some congress leagues present a Sweepstakes Award at the end of the season.

Most often, the judges who are assigned to the final session for each chamber oversee the balloting for awards. The tabulation room provides a list of nominations for the outstanding and superior speakers, the best presiding officer, and the best legislation. The judges list the nominees on the board and conduct a vote for each category. This is usually done by a paper-ballot vote. The NFL *Student Congress Manual* recommends the following procedure for balloting:

> When using the ballot vote (and not the
> preferential voting process), each member,
> including the presiding officer, shall
> on each ballot vote for one nominee.
> After each ballot, unless one candidate
> has received a majority of the votes cast,
> the person receiving the fewest votes
> shall be dropped. If the combined votes
> of the two lowest candidates do not equal
> the votes of the next lowest candidate,
> both shall be eliminated. If there is a
> tie for the lowest two or three candidates,
> it is recommended that a vote be taken on
> the tied candidates and eliminate only one
> candidate at a time. [4]

When the balloting is complete the judges send the results to the tabulation room for recording. Once this is done, an awards ceremony is held to recognize the winning students. In addition to the presentation of awards, a packet of tournament results is presented to each school. The tabulation sheets along with the legislative critique sheets are included (see Appendix). The sheets indicate how well each student performed in competition. Coaches and sponsors can use the result sheets to record participation points with the NFL.

Summary

In this chapter we have highlighted the mechanics of the Student Congress operation. Our discussion has focused on committee and legislative sessions, presiding officer responsibilities, parliamentary procedure, critic judge responsibilities, Student Congress politics, and voting procedures. In discussing the mechanics of Student Congress we have largely been influenced by our participation in Student Congress in the Midwest and the NFL National Student Congress. We acknowledge that customs may vary from one place to another. However, all Student Congress competitions have many things in common. It is basically an interscholastic speech event whereby students make most of the decisions in legislative sessions chaired by a presiding officer.

Notes

1. David Mezzera and John Giertz, *Student Congress and Lincoln-Douglas Debate* (Lincolnwood, Ill.: National Textbook Company, 1991), 22–23.

2. Henry M. Robert and Susan Corbin Robert, *Robert's Rules of Order Newly Revised* (Glenview, Ill.: Scott, Foresman, 1990).

3. *Student Congress Manual,* 5.

4. Ibid., 7.

Discussion Questions

1. Discuss the relative merits of apportioning legislative chambers to include students with similar experience and background and students with varied experience and background.

2. What factors should govern the work of committees that meet to select bills and resolutions for debate?

3. What is the rationale for alternating speeches, pro and con, and for recognizing legislators who have not spoken before recognizing a speaker for a second time?

4. Discuss the characteristics of a good presiding officer.

5. Why is adherence to parliamentary procedure in Student Congress necessary?

6. Discuss the differences between main, subsidiary, incidental, and privileged motions.

7. What role does the critic judge play in Student Congress?

8. Should students engage in "playing politics"? Why or why not?

9. Discuss the ramifications of students competing against each other making decisions on most awards to be presented.

Appendix

Sample Congress Invitation

December 10

Dear Student Congress Coach:

The Valley High School Discussion and Debate Team cordially invites you and your debaters to attend a Student Congress competition on Friday and Saturday, January 24–25. The competition will be scheduled for both Friday and Saturday (please see enclosed schedule). Student Congress legislation will be mailed to any school that did not attend the Streamwood Congress December 13–14.

The enclosed registration form indicating the number of student representatives attending with level of experience and committee preference must be received by January 17. Houses will be proportioned by levels of experience and sweepstakes at this tournament will be determined by the highest average point total, per student, per school. To be eligible for sweepstakes awards, each school must have at least one representative per chamber.

Entry fees can accompany your registration form or can be paid at registration January 24. The cost will be $4 per congressperson. Each school will be responsible for one congress judge for each eight participants.

We look forward to seeing you in 1993! If any questions arise, please call.

Sincerely,

Joan Marcus

Ed Brown

Joan Marcus
Ed Brown
Coaches

Schedule of Events—Student Congress

Friday, January 24

Registration	4:30 p.m.– 5:00 p.m.
Committee Sessions	5:15 p.m.– 5:45 p.m.
Dinner	6:00 p.m.– 6:30 p.m.
Session I	6:30 p.m.– 9:00 p.m.

Saturday, January 25

Session II	8:30 a.m.–11:00 a.m.
Lunch	11:00 a.m.–12:00 noon
Session III	12:15 p.m.– 2:45 p.m.
Elections	3:00 p.m.– 3:45 p.m.
Awards	4:00 p.m.

Valley High School Student Congress
Registration Form

School _____   Coach _____
Street _____   School Phone _____
City _____   Home Phone _____

Congress Contestant	Yrs. Exp.	Committee
1.		
2.		
3.		
4.		
5.		
6.		
7.		
8.		
9.		
10.		
11.		
12.		
13.		
14.		
15.		
16.		
17.		
18.		
19.		
20.		

Registration Totals

Congress Participants_____ × $4 = _____

TOTAL DUE = _____

Legislative Chamber Assignment with Committee Appointment

CHAMBER 4   Room 452   Blue

School	Participant	Committee	
PHS	Jason Wicklander	EC	Committees will meet in
	Chris Katsoulis	FA	the Chamber Room.
DHS	Sean Roland	PW	Committee Chairs
	Beth Goltzer	FA	should return com-
			mittee result forms to
			room 444.
LT	Bob Oppenheim	PW	People who switch
	Jenny Praser	EC	chambers without
			a coach's permission
			will not have results
			tabbed.
DC	Susanna Diaz	FA*	
LF	Elvin Day	FA	
	Sara Brown	PW	
	Peter Brugemann (Fri.)	FA	
STWD	Aaron Compton	EC	
RM	Tina Rau (Sat.)	EC	
HP	Carly Herz	EC*	
	Debra Mitsui	PW	
	Justin Rosen	FA	
	Darrell Friel	PW	
WHS	Jeff Cohen	PW*	
	Regina Bass	PW	
STC	Mike Lawson	EC	
	Laura Houk	FA	
	Sanjay Ramakrishna	PW	

*Committee Chairs

Committee Report

Chamber _____ Committee _____

We have chosen the following bills to be debated in the following order:

1. _____

2. _____

3. _____

4. _____

_____
Signature of Committee Chairperson

Please return this form to the tab room (room 444). Committee results need to be written on blackboard in each chamber. Results will be posted outside room 444 as well.

Tabulation Sheet—
Legislative Session

CHAMBER I   ROOM 152

School	Participant	I.	II.	Subtotal	III.	Total
SC	Lesniak, J.	1		1	0	1
SC	Neville, P.	44 6	4 3	21	2 4	27
SC	Swensen, K.	2	2	4	1	5
HP	Schiffer, J.	23 6	1 4	16	2 4	22
HP	Wrobel, B.	2	5 4	11	5 5	21
HP	Chavez, A.	5 4	4 3	16	2	18
HP	Rosen, D.	53 6	454 6	33	54 6	48
NT	Waltman, A.	4 5	P07 15	24	5 6	35
NT	Bekin, B.	2 4	3 3	12	4 4	20
RM	Ailes, Kristin	1	3 3	7	2 2	11
RM	Kim, N.	44 6	5443 6	36	45 6	50
DC	Nakamura, M.	32 5	311 5	20	33 5	31
DC	Huff, J.	1	2	3	3	6
JH	Gliecki, M.	3	2 4	9	3	11
JH	Zolotoff, M.	2	2	4	0	4
AU	Hadley, A.	2	2 2	6	1	7
AU	Jorjorian, N.	0	1	1	3 2	6
PR	Patel, B.	3	34 5	15	3 3	21
PR	Interrante, C.	3 4	2	9	3 3	15
PR	Chambliss, T.	P09 13	4 4	21	4 5	30

Judges' Nomination for Outstanding Speaker

CHAMBER _____

SESSION: 1   2   3   (circle)

1. Speaker _____ School _____

2. Speaker _____ School _____

Please list the bills debated this session.

1. _____ # _____

2. _____ # _____

3. _____ # _____

4. _____ # _____

Judges _____   _____

Each judge should choose one delegate. Consider speeches, questions answered and asked, and general participation. Compare choices. If you have chosen the same student, choose a second nominee.

Presiding officer this session was _____.

After the conclusion of the session, please assign participation points (0–6) and write them on a seating chart. One judge should bring the P.O. critique form, any ballots, the participation points, and this form to the tab room (room 444).

Thank you.

Presiding Officer Critique Form

Name _____

Chamber _____ Session _____

Qualifications:

1. Presiding officer should demonstrate knowledge of parliamentary procedure.
2. Presiding officer should be fair in selecting speakers.
3. Presiding officer should be able to maintain order.
4. Presiding officer should be able to keep the debate flowing.
5. Presiding officer should be poised.

Comments:

Points Awarded: 10   9   8   7   6   5   4   3   2   1

Judge _____ Judge _____

School _____ School _____

Legislative Speech Critique Form

Name _____ School _____ Session _____ Chamber _____

Legislation # _____ Pro _____ Con _____

Standards for Excellence:
1. The speaker's introduction gains attention and defines his or her stand.
2. The speaker extends debate by:
    (a) referring to and refuting previous argument;
    (b) referring to and extending previous argument;
    (c) summarizing and introducing new argument.
3. The speaker's arguments are clearly stated, logical, fully developed, and reasonably supported.
4. The speaker is poised, uses language effectively, and demonstrates extemporaneous style.
5. The speaker demonstrates confidence and a full understanding of topic area when answering questions in the aftermath of the speech.

Comments:

Speaker's overall ability: Superior   Excellent   Good   Fair
Points Awarded: 6   5   4   3   2   1

Critic's Signature _____

Glossary

Abstain   To refrain from something by one's own choice, as to abstain from voting.

Abstract   A type of index that gives the location of an article in a periodical or a book and a brief summary of the article.

Advocate   A person who seeks to persuade others to accept his or her position in a debate.

Alternate Cause   A factor that may explain an event that was not considered in developing a causal argument.

Ambiguous   A term that may be subject to more than one meaning; vague and unclear.

Amendment   A formal proposal to change a bill or resolution to improve its debatability.

Analogy   The use of comparison to draw a strong general conclusion.

Analysis   Systematic research that leads to an understanding of the topic under consideration.

Argument   A discussion in which disagreement is expressed about some point; a course of reasoning aimed at demonstrating the truth of a point; a claim supported by evidence and reasoning.

Argumentation   The study of the process of forming reasons to justify controversial claims.

Article   A piece of writing that is part of a larger work.

Assertion   A statement without supporting evidence.

Attack   The refutation of an opponent's position.

Audience Analysis   The process of determining what evidence and reasoning an audience will accept.

Authority   An acknowledged expert in a particular field.

Authorship Speech   Speech that opens debate on a bill or resolution, usually made by the person who wrote the legislation.

Ballot   A sheet of paper on which a vote is registered; act or process of voting; total number of votes cast in an election.

Benefit   An advantage that comes from pursuing a course of action.

Best Legislation   The bill or resolution that Student Congress participants determine to be the best submitted for debate.

Bibliography   A list of sources of information: books, periodicals, newspapers, etc.

Bill   A legislative proposal formally introduced for consideration; becomes law if enacted.

Brainstorming   A process used to develop a list of debatable topics or to explore a topic to discover arguments.

Brief   An outline of an argument with supporting evidence and reasoning.

Call to Order   Presiding officer formally opens a legislative session.

Card Catalogue   An alphabetical listing of all books in a library.

Causal Argument   An argument in which one event or idea is said to have an influence on another event or idea.

CD-ROM Database stored on a compact disc and accessed by a computer (compact disc–read only memory).

Chamber Room in which legislative body meets and conducts business.

Claim An assertion you want your audience to accept.

Clash A direct response to an opposing argument.

Committee A body of legislators officially delegated to select the best legislation to be debated.

Concurrent Resolution A special measure passed by one house of Congress with the other house concurring; used to make or amend joint rules or to express the sentiment of Congress on some issue or event.

Con Speech A three-minute speech in which one opposes a bill or resolution.

Contention A major point (claim) of a case.

Copyright The legal right to control production, use, and sale of copies of a literary, musical, or artistic work.

Credibility Trust accorded a source of information; trust accorded a speaker by the audience.

Critic Person who judges student performance and evaluates that performance.

Critique Sheet A form used by the critic judge to convey the evaluation of student speeches.

Database Units of information that are stored in machine-readable form and retrieved by use of a computer.

Defense The support of a position that has been attacked by an opponent.

Disadvantage An unwanted and undesirable consequence of taking a course of action.

Documentation Citing the source of information used.

Election The act of choosing by vote among candidates to fill a position.

Enforcement   Mandated steps to be taken to ensure that actions called for in a bill are followed.

Evidence   Information used to support a claim; the foundation on which an argument rests.

Expert   A person who by training and experience is knowledgeable about a specific subject.

Extemporaneous   To deliver a speech that is not read or committed to memory.

Extend   Adding new insight and evidence to support a previously made argument.

Eye Contact   Looking at the audience while speaking to determine their reactions to you and your message.

Fact   A statement that is objectively verifiable.

Flowchart   A sheet of paper set up to take notes of arguments made by speakers in a legislative session.

Generalization   A general conclusion warranted by specific instances.

Harms   Undesirable consequences of an action called for in a bill or resolution.

Implement   To pass into law.

Inference   A mental operation that links evidence to a claim.

Infotrac   A computer-based listing of library resources (Information Access Company).

Issue   An argument inherent in and vital to the acceptance or rejection of a controversial topic.

Joint Resolution   A congressional action that requires the approval of both houses and has the force of law if approved.

Journal   Scholarly periodical usually issued monthly or quarterly.

Key Terms   Important words or phrases in a bill or resolution that need to be defined in order for debate to proceed.

Keyword Searching   Online catalogue searching using nonstandardized subject headings.

Legislative Session   A formal period of time during which a legislative body debates.

Majority   The number of votes which constitutes one more than half the total.

Methodology   The logical principles or procedural steps taken in conducting a study.

Motion   A call for a vote in Student Congress.

Nomination   The act of submitting a name for an office to be filled by vote or appointment.

Online Catalogue   Library catalogue records in a machine-readable form that are accessed by use of computers.

Online Search   A search that is carried out by means of a computer.

Opinion   A statement that includes a judgment about reality.

Outstanding Speaker   The student who receives the highest number of votes.

Parliamentarian   A person who is an expert in the accepted rules and procedures in a legislature; advises the presiding officer on technical questions and advises the chamber when inquiries about procedure are raised.

Parliamentary Procedure   The body of rules generally accepted as appropriate for the conduct of legislative affairs.

Presiding Officer   The student who is elected to preside over the legislative chamber during a debate session.

Previous Question   A motion ''to move the previous question,'' when adopted, ends debate by a required vote. A two-thirds vote is required.

Primary Source   A firsthand or eyewitness account.

Privileged Motion   A motion in a legislative body that must be considered ahead of other motions.

Probability   The odds that an event will occur.

Pro Speech   A three-minute speech in favor of the pending legislation.

Rating   A numerical score awarded by the critic judge for participation in the debate.

Recess   A cessation of the customary activities of a legislative session.

Refutation   The process of exposing weaknesses in arguments.

Research   Investigation and study in some field of knowledge to establish facts or principles.

Resolution   A congressional resolution offers the sense of the legislature but does not carry the force of law.

Risk   The probability that future action will produce undesirable consequences.

Seating Chart   A diagram of student seating arrangement that allows the presiding officer, members of the chamber, and the critic judge to identify members of a chamber.

Secondary Source   Literature that analyzes, interprets, relates, or evaluates a primary source or other secondary sources.

Stock Issues   Ill: What is the nature, scope and significance of the problem? Blame: What causes the problem? Cure: What is needed to solve the problem? Cost: What risk is involved in taking the action?

Subsidiary Motion   Secondary motion.

Superior Speaker   The student legislator who receives the second highest vote total.

Sweepstakes Award   A trophy or other award for the team (school) that does best at a tournament or at the end of a series of tournaments.

Tabulation Room   A place where tournament coordinators collect and record information necessary to operate the tournament.

Testimony   Primary type of evidence used in Student Congress competition.

Toulmin Model   A model of an argument (unit of proof) that allows students to visualize the relationship between evidence, inference, and claim.

Transition   Serves to connect major lines of analysis. Tells the audience that you are concluding one major idea and are moving to the next major idea.

Value Claim   Judgmental claim that attempts to assign positive or negative worth to an object of evaluation.

Word Economy   The use of as few words as possible to make an idea clear and convincing.

Index